Phil M. Wagler

Kingdom
CULTURE

Growing the Missional Church

KINGDOM CULTURE
Growing the Missional Church

Cover photography by Jen Wagler.

Printed in Canada.

ISBN-10: 1-897373-99-6
ISBN-13: 978-1-897373-99-6

Printed by Word Alive Press
131 Cordite Road, Winnipeg, MB R3W 1S1
www.wordalivepress.ca

WORD ALIVE PRESS
Just Write!

For Jen.

ENDORSEMENTS

"Reading this book is like sitting with Phil Wagler at a table—which I have done many times. You warm to his love of the church, his candor, and the depth of his theology. In Kingdom Culture, Wagler now illuminates the discussion of the missional church by pastoral experience. I recommend it to church leaders to inspire and re-focus in a Biblical direction."

CARSON PUE, PRESIDENT, ARROW LEADERSHIP
AND AUTHOR OF MENTORING LEADERS: WISDOM FOR
DEVELOPING CHARACTER, CALLING AND COMPETENCY

"If more churches and more pastors could help to generate more disciples with this kind of vision for the kingdom, the world would be a much better place... The unlikelihood that an Almighty deity would entrust the keys of the Kingdom to such as us is at the very heart of the Christian calling. This book helps us come to terms with that reality and guides us into deeper spiritual truth and action."

DOUG KOOP, EDITORIAL DIRECTOR
CHRISTIANWEEK

"Phil Wagler gives the church a guidebook that has childlike simplicity, is deeply profound... The engaging parables and practical ideas in the "toolbox" make this a serious offering for any leader or group of leaders praying for the transformation of their congregation. Kingdom Culture is already in my denominational toolbox."

BRIAN BAUMAN, MISSION MINISTER
MENNONITE CHURCH EASTERN CANADA.

"The word 'missional' is more than a buzzword. In Kingdom Culture, you will find that it is the passion of a man who longs to see God's people mobilized for the greatest adventure on planet earth. As Jesus taught

ENDORSEMENTS

us, Phil prays, "Thy kingdom come." Then he puts feet to those prayers. This book challenges us all to walk the talk."
DAVE BROWNING, LEAD PASTOR
CHRIST THE KING COMMUNITY CHURCH INTERNATIONAL

"This book is a love letter to the church... the language is tough, the tone hopeful. Wagler's incisive and unflinching analysis reminds us of what we've often forgotten, that God is for the world. This is a workbook, best consumed and digested in community. A helpful tool for congregations to discern God's call to them."
NORM VOTH, DIRECTOR OF EVANGELISM AND SERVICE MINISTRIES
MENNONITE CHURCH MANITOBA

"Phil brings the missional church down from the stratosphere of ideas and into the hurly-burly of everyday life."
JAMES WATSON, CHURCH PLANTING CANADA NATIONAL TEAM

"If you are not sure what a 'missional' congregation is, don't worry. By the end, you will be much clearer on this 'messy' concept and motivated to try new approaches in your own setting."
MELODIE DAVIS, AUTHOR/EDITOR
THIRD WAY CAFÉ, ANOTHER WAY

"Never have I read a work that blended history into such meaningful lessons for today's church. This book helps centre church leaders on what matters most and gives practical tools to guide the avid learner."
RYAN ERB, DIRECTOR OF INSTITUTIONAL ADVANCEMENT
EMMANUEL BIBLE COLLEGE

"Phil Wagler has produced a book that has the ability to radically change the direction of your ministry."
GERALD REIMER, CONFERENCE YOUTH MINISTER
EVANGELICAL MENNONITE CONFERENCE

"This book radiates the love of Jesus."
TROY WATSON, PASTOR/SPIRITUAL LIFE DIRECTOR
QUEST COMMUNITY CHURCH

ACKNOWLEDGEMENTS

Now, whatever you do, do not skip these acknowledgements, or you will miss some very important people whom you will want to meet when you get to heaven.

My deep gratitude goes to my church family, Kingsfield (Zurich Mennonite & Clinton), for their courage in truly living and embracing life in Christ and the challenge of these four declarations. I also appreciate their love for my family. These amazing saints have, for over one hundred years, been a consistent and creative witness of the resurrected Lord. They humble and teach me. Special thanks to Ian and Val, for making their wonderful garden cottage available as the perfect place to think, pray, and write, and to Evan Braun for his editorial insights.

To my friends Tom, Ryan, Randy, Tim, Jamie, and Damian—thanks for challenging me, stretching me, and sharing your thoughts and correctives to this project.

To my mentors Virgil and Victor—thanks for lending your experience, wisdom, honesty, and love for Jesus and his people to my life.

Thanks to my mom and dad—I owe you more than you will ever realize, including an incredible optimism and perseverance.

Most importantly, to my beautiful bride Jen whose innocence, purity, and determination has been a picture for me of what the bride of Christ can be. We have lived much in a short time—thanks for taking me with you on the journey.

And then there are my greatest cheerleaders and fiercest critics—Caleb, Benjamin, Jessie, and Sadie—thank you for reminding me that my mission is first and foremost to be lived with and for you.

Let the Kingdom come...

- PHIL WAGLER

INTRODUCTION

There was a day when I never read the introduction to a book. It seemed like an enormous waste of my infinitely valuable time. Introductions are for those with too much time on their hands, or perhaps for people on holiday. They could also be fine distractions if you're waiting in a dental office listening to the fearful buzz of a drill drifting out of the next room and you need something, anything, to keep your mind off the inevitable.

Things have changed, however. Perhaps it's a sign of approaching maturity, but I now take the time, always, to read an author's opening comments. This is because I realize, even more so as I contemplated writing this work, that a writer has much they *need* to say before they can say what they *want* to say. In addition, introductions give me a window, be it ever so small, into the world of an author whose insights and perspective I am about to ingest and digest, and even use to adjust my ways. So, I do hope you take the time to read these preliminary thoughts and I pray that you not come to regret having invested the time in the exercise of ingesting and digesting what follows.

This work comes from my heart and my experience of the Church as a mid-thirties Generation X follower of Jesus Christ, church leader, son, husband, and father. I have lived my life in the shadows of church building doors for as long as I can remember. Uncomfortable pews have been my hind-numbing reality for too many years—which may go a long way in explaining the abundant padding that is apparent in my rear view mirror. Or maybe it was all those potlucks and mandatory Sunday afternoon naps. In any event, the body of Christ has been an antagonist, a frustration, and a passion for me. It took both a short and long time to embrace this paradox. The bride is both beautiful and bewildering, but I still love her.

Be careful, however, not to misunderstand me at this crucial point. I love the Church because she is God's creation, because of His vision for her, but not because of what religious humanity has made of her. G.K. Chesterton once said insightfully that "Christianity has not so much been tried and found wanting, as it has been found difficult and left untried." The same could be said of the Church. In truth, it seems to me that the Church—from which many in my generation are fleeing, and yet still curiously circle like seagulls at a beach picnic—has not so much been tried and found wanting, as she has been difficult and left untried. This is what this book is meant to address.

It is my purpose to lend my voice, for whatever it is worth, to the chorus of those more wise than I who in each generation call the Body of Christ to stay in shape and embrace the outrageous call to be a people set apart in this wonderful, woesome world as a radically different community, a wild-space, a holy nation of God's Kingdom princes and princesses who engage the times, the culture, and the Church with focus and fervour.

The Kingdom culture declarations you will read in the pages that follow are meant to embody in practical terms the missional existence of the Church. "Missional" is a trendy word these days for churches and their leaders, but is often about as well-understood as quantum physics is by ordinary sheep just looking for a good flock to graze with during this ideological, perplexing, and experientially diverse post-Christian age.

It was because we in my home church in Huron County, Ontario were becoming conversant in this new postmodern "Christianese" that we saw the need to describe missional in action terms. What good is it to say we are missional if no one knows what it means and must first take a course in order to do so? Why waste time getting people to speak missionally when what we really desire is for them to *live* missionally? These were the questions that led to the development of these declarations by our rural Canadian fellowship of believers.

Before you begin, however, you must understand that these declarations do not replace sound orthodoxy (sound doctrine), but rather spring from an individual and corporate commitment to that apostolic faith which has been handed down through the ages that declares Jesus Christ to be the Son of God, the incarnated Word of

God made flesh, who was crucified, died, buried, and rose from the dead to fulfill what was written about him in the First Testament Scriptures. Jesus' invitation to all people is to repent of sin and life on our own terms, follow him alone as Lord and Leader in faith, and live faithfully in the world by God's grace in the power of the Holy Spirit as a member of the mysterious Body of Christ until death do you *not* separate. The Apostle's Creed and our confessions of faith as summaries of the biblical witness guide our orthodoxy and are essential foundations for our orthopraxis—the sound practice of the Christ-centered life.

My concern for some of what is emerging in the Church these days is an overemphasis on *praxis* as the only viable expression of Church without an equal appreciation for the necessity of the soundness of doctrine. Both are foundational and required elements in this divine intervention and, as in other periods of history, we risk cutting off the limb we stand on once more if we do not keep both truth and practice as dancing partners.

The four missional Kingdom culture declarations we now proclaim are things we are getting into the habit of saying in my home church fellowship. This does not imply we become effective missional communities simply by saying so. Far too many congregations have developed pithy mission and vision slogans that have never become practical realities. In the end, such "re-visioning" can simply give a false sense of accomplishment. We return to business as usual. At the same time, what we say about ourselves is critically important. So we say these declarations in the same way that we say our names—because it is who we are. When we speak of a missional Kingdom culture, we are identifying our very nature as the body of Christ in the world. We are reminding ourselves that sometimes this is not how we are behaving and that we must once again return to our purpose, practice, and true identity.

The four declarations are not set in hierarchical order, but should be read as carrying equal weight and importance, each as necessary as the four corners of a foundation. In my opinion, these four missional emphases are not only biblical and sourced in the only foundation that can be laid, Jesus Christ (1 Corinthians 3:11), but they describe the balanced base upon which the healthy internal and external life of the Church in any age can be built.

A story or parable will introduce each statement in order to prepare the mind, heart, and imagination for their force and impact. Each declaration will then be defined in two digestible portions with reflective questions for further review in order to encourage you, your small group, or leadership team to dig deeper into your own context and cultural realities, to which you have been called to be the Church.

At the end of each section there will be some tools that we have found helpful in our context to grow us as a people who let the Kingdom come. There are, of course, a myriad of resources available these days, but I share these particular ones as options and recommendations, not prescriptions. In reading a work like this, we can very easily skip over such tools in order to get the book finished and move on. Yet the value of this exercise you are about to engage will be markedly higher if you take the time, especially in group or leadership team settings, to use the tools to open your eyes and hearts to the Spirit's work among you.

TABLE OF CONTENTS

CHAPTER ONE

"No One Gets Left Behind"

Let the Kingdom Come...

Saturday morning dawned with cool, clear beauty. An excited gaggle of fifty men and boys descended upon Bruce Peninsula National Park in Ontario for a Father's Day weekend excursion. I'm no scientist, but I would venture to guess that the energy level packed into our jalopy bus for the ride north on Friday night was somewhere close to that of enriched uranium.

Our mission as men was to facilitate much-needed inter-generational testosterone time and wear out the next generation with as little loss of life and limb as possible. So, when the sun rose on the first morning, there was excitement amid the satisfying, greasy aroma of bacon and eggs drifting through the air.

Even though most of the boys had not laid head to pillow before midnight, the campsite was a scurry of activity before seven bells. Sticks were swinging, balls were flying, forest forts were under construction, insects were under investigation, and trails and lakes required exploration before the breakfast call went out.

Slowly, if not reluctantly, the boys returned to inhale chicken and pig, storing up the necessary reserves for a big day of hiking and rock climbing. With such a large crowd bustling about like bugs beneath an overturned log, it was quite difficult to know who was and was not present. As a result, it was quite some time before anyone noticed that Josiah was missing.

"Have you seen Josiah?" his dad asked.

"No, I haven't, but he was with..."

And so we continued serving breakfast and keeping our eyes open for the six-year-old's return with the next wave of critters who returned to camp. However, as

*the kids who had apparently last been with Josiah returned to the trough one by one,
it became clear that no one could remember seeing him recently at all.*

*Josiah's dad and a handful of others began hurrying down nearby trails calling
out his name.*

They heard back nothing...but racing hearts.

*Meanwhile, back at the camp, life was proceeding as if nothing was wrong at
all. Some were doing dishes, some were back to stick fighting with bacon grease on
their lips, and others were getting a picnic lunch packed. By now, everyone had heard
that Josiah was nowhere to be found.*

*Finally, after about a half-hour, an uncommon panic began to set in among
men who are used to being lost and not asking for directions. They must have figured
that little Josiah was simply doing what males do and would either eventually find
his way back or at worst bump into a woman who would tell him where to go.*

*I had been down a few trails by this point, met several hikers who had not seen a
single soul, and returned to the campsite empty-handed, increasingly aggravated by
the apparent apathy of those chewing their bacon and buttering their bread as if
nothing of importance was happening. One of our own was missing, a dad was
sweating buckets, and it seemed many were oblivious and indifferent, even though
they knew what all the hustle and bustle was about.*

*As I pondered this, our brave and probably medicated bus driver walked by and
said, "Someone should organize a search party."*

*Internally, I had been wrestling for a while with a sense that we should gather
everyone together, halt the exuberance that was keeping us from focusing on the real
task at hand, and pray for Josiah's safety and return. I sensed this, but had not done
anything more than run a few trails and ask a few questions on my own or with
another willing partner. The time had come to mobilize.*

*By now, Josiah had not been seen or heard from for at least an hour. Call us
tardy, but we finally gathered, organized, and prayed for Josiah—wherever he might
be on those trails with cliff drop-offs, rattlesnakes, and who knows who or what else.*

*When we finished praying, we began to map out a plan. No children would be
permitted to leave the campsite until Josiah was found. Men would be sent out in
pairs, covering all the paths he might possibly have ventured down with two-way
radios in hand. The park warden's office would be called, but mothers would not
be—at least not yet. The urgency, camaraderie, and emerging giftedness were*

inspiring and I began to wonder what rock this unbridled passion had been hiding under.

And then, about five minutes after we had prayed, and just as we were about to embark on our coordinated and daring rescue, down the north path of our group site and through the trees emerged a young couple with a small red-sweatered lad in tow. Josiah had been found.

His eyes were puffy and red from crying. A cheer of celebration arose spontaneously from grandpas, fathers, and three-year-olds alike, and radio connection was made to ease dad's high blood pressure. Soon the two were in each other's arms in a prodigal-son-come-home embrace.

Josiah would tell us that he had become separated from the other boys and then headed in the wrong direction on a trail that would have led him to camp. Scared and realizing he was lost, he eventually sat down, cried, and prayed for someone to find him. Shortly thereafter, the hiking couple had come across him. Having been told earlier to keep their eyes open for a little boy in a red sweater, they abandoned their own hike to return this little lost lamb to the fold.

Saturday definitely turned out spectacularly beautiful.

My experience with this group of brothers became, only in retrospect, a parable for me of the way many Christians interact with others—even those who are seemingly part of the fold.

Many of us are keenly aware that some people are disoriented in life, left behind, hurting and wounded, headed in a wrong direction, or conspicuous by their absence, and yet very few seem engaged in the process of bringing them home.

There are a few scurrying about, even panicked, as they seek to embrace people—and generally it is assumed that this is what we pay pastors to do—but by and large many are simply busy enjoying the campsite, grease on their lips, wondering what all the fuss is about. We have left the embracing of people to programs that by their very nature become bureaucratic and cumbersome over time, despite their good intentions. Content that "the Church," supported by our offerings, is doing something, many followers of Jesus never conduct a meaningful search for another human being that involves any semblance of personal sacrifice. In fact, they haven't done so in such a long time that they come to believe it cannot be done, or at the very least that it requires a theological degree. Many would not even be aware of how effective, or ineffective, the programs they hold so dear really are at embracing and rescuing people made in the image of God.

Furthermore, we have lost sight of the reality that there are untold scores of Josiahs parked on stumps, hoping and praying for someone to find them, to notice them, to lead them somewhere—anywhere other than where they are. The harvest is great, declared Jesus to his disciples, but the workers are few (Matthew 9:37).

And that leads to another surprising lesson from our camp parable. It can be the case that while we enjoy our camp songs in secluded harmony, there are others doing the finding for us who are not part of us. Or so we think.

It is time for the followers of Jesus to live with the conviction that no one gets left behind.

A KINGDOM CULTURE THAT SEES PEOPLE

*And the LORD said, "You pity the plant, for which you did not
labor, nor did you make it grow, which came into being in a
night and perished in a night. And should not I pity Nineveh,
that great city, in which there are more than 120,000 persons
who do not know their right hand from their left, and also much
cattle?"*

JONAH 4:10-11

Be kind, for everyone you meet is fighting a great battle.

PHILO OF ALEXANDRIA

The prophet Jonah is a tragic Old Testament figure. This messenger
of the Living God tried much and endured much in his ill-fated bid
to rid himself of the presence of the LORD. Actually, he was really
running away from the compassion and mercy of God only to
experience how deep that love actually goes. The great fish, the vomit,
the plant, and even the worm that destroyed his cherished vine were all
expressions of the grace-filled nature of the Living God.

Jonah was a prophet. He spoke for God. He knew God. He knew
God took note of wickedness and would not stand unrighteousness—
at least not in other people. And he knew God's gracious heart. In fact,
the unwelcome invitation to do a speaking tour of greater Nineveh was
proof that God's justice is guided by astounding mercy. Where people
are perishing, God acts. This God does not play favourites.

Furthermore, and this Jonah simply did not or would not grasp,
God is determined that human beings who share his image also share
his compassionate nature for one another and all God's creatures, even
across ethnic and national lines. Hence Jonah's command to go was not
the opportunity for a fun cross-cultural short-term mission experience.
He would not simply spend a few days immersed in Assyrian culture,
taste the peculiar food, and bring home some cool souvenirs and a few
lingual phrases like "Thank you for not putting a fish hook in my
mouth" (the Assyrians were infamous for such brutal treatment of their
enemies). This prophetic tour was meant to be the embodiment of the

nature of the God he knew and spoke for. God is compassionate and merciful—Jonah knew as much—and the Israelite was to be the poster boy of that divine reality in downtown Gentile Nineveh. Jonah was to be a sign that the true God was determined to leave no one behind. Instead, he ran in the opposite direction. When he finally does comply, it seems only for the sadistic pleasure of being able to watch *Sodom and Gommorah: The Sequel*.

Too often Jonah is simply remembered for his biblical venture into the world of marine biology. The focal point of the story, however, is the open-ended way in which the story ends. The story is really about Jonah and the plant. Jonah loves his creature comforts, is selfishly satisfied with having performed his prophetic religious duty obediently, but the whole thing remains one huge adventure in missing the point.

God loves people. Even God's righteous judgment is really about his aching love for men and women, girls and boys. In the same way that a good parent's anger is a mark of their deep love and compassion, God's love will sometimes be uncomfortable. But it is love nonetheless—radical, exuberant, selfless, abounding love. Love never fails. Such is the love of God shared with us and which we who know him are asked to live in our backyard, our Nineveh, and beyond.

Karl Barth, the Swiss theologian whose voice guided the Church through some of the most trying circumstances of the twentieth century, challenged us to think about our relationships with other people and their cultures with this guiding question, "What will happen to the people?" Jonah ought to have asked this. Instead, Nineveh became for him one large theatre in which he could watch with detachment and self-righteous glee a Hollywood-like action blockbuster. Nineveh would be pummelled and he would have a front row seat. "What will happen to the people?" was simply not part of the equation. The possibility that these "pagans" might actually heed the word of the Lord and repent never seems to enter his consciousness. He did his duty and preached his unwilling message: Bring on the brimstone!

But the Assyrians do the unthinkable! They repent. Even their animals are sorry. And God's heart softens. God's love wins out. The

Lord gratefully relents. This simply does not suit Jonah's fancy. His fun is ruined. His front row seat turns out to be a supreme rip-off. His shade disappears and his body and heart are fully exposed. Grace and second chances were his food, but no one else is allowed a seat at the table.

Hence, the episode comes to a close with the startling word of the Lord, "Shouldn't I feel sorry for such a great city?" Jonah's actions betray that he believed he knew better than God. He assumed God saw the world through the eyes of the prophet. From God's perspective, however, things looked much different. For God, it really is about the people, leaving us to ponder the implications for centuries to come, including our own day, when terrorists and villains of all stripes are striking fear and hate once more.

To be a missional *ecclesia*, to be the called-out Church on mission from God, requires more than the performance of our religious duties and the implementation of trendy programs that will somehow bring success or breathe life into our dry bones. As with Jonah, our congregational life, in all its various programmatic expressions, takes the place of our ability to see people. When this happens, we find ourselves perched with the prophet beneath the withering, worm-full plant.

Ironically, many congregations continue to beat the drum on forms and patterns of ministry that have almost entirely lost touch with people. We're busy doing and running "church stuff"—or at least what we have become accustomed to institutional churches doing—but we have ceased seeing people. Many churches are still driving programmatic Studebakers while our neighbours and culture have moved on to Smart Cars. They gaze upon the vintage models we service and chug by on with a nostalgia reserved for heritage shows.

In our community, the end of August sees a huge vintage car drive-by and tour. People line the streets to watch restored and polished vehicles of yesteryear paraded by. It strikes me that many in our postmodern culture view the church in much the same way. We parade our programs in front of them, ask them to jump on board if they can squeeze in, but our focus is the old car and not the people. In the end, we are simply just another social service provider, or worse, entertainment source.

Furthermore, and this is even more troubling, we only know our brothers and sisters in Christ in the context of our Studebakers. We can hardly imagine that this passage from Acts is even possible:

> *And they devoted themselves to the apostles' teaching and fellowship, to the breaking of bread and the prayers. And awe came upon every soul, and many wonders and signs were being done through the apostles. And all who believed were together and had all things in common. And they were selling their possessions and belongings and distributing the proceeds to all, as any had need. And day by day, attending the temple together and breaking bread in their homes, they received their food with glad and generous hearts, praising God and having favor with all the people. And the Lord added to their number day by day those who were being saved.*
>
> ACTS 2:42-47

The focus of the Christ-centered life of the early church was God and people. This vision was rooted in that what they had experienced of Jesus. In his company, they beheld God's lavish love and the full attention given people. Because they knew God the Father saw people first, because of their own incredible transforming experience of the risen Jesus, and because of the Holy Spirit's work to bring God and people together, they saw people first and foremost. These first disciples were characterized by their commitment to truth, to experiencing life together, to eating together and seeking God's will together in prayer. Money and possessions were blessings and responsibilities to be shared. Need was known because people were known. Being together in big and small groups brought joy—and a threat to the powers that be. Miracles happened. Worship was simply the heart of all this living together. Favour with people of all stripes was the reality. And gloriously, lives entered the whole salvation of God in increasing measure.

What is striking in this brief summary of the honeymoon days of the Church is the harmonic presence of orthodoxy (sound and true teaching) and orthopraxy (sound and true practice) and how both were central to seeing people accurately. Truth opens eyes to see people as beautiful *and* broken beings. The truth in Christ awakens a wonder at the miracle of the human being made in God's image and it awakens a sorrow at the way this miracle has been ravaged by sin. Experiencing resurrected life in Christ causes us to see and love well, as God sees and loves.

To be missional, therefore, means to recover a commitment to the apostolic message and develop the ability to see humanity once more, to see those who have yet to know Christ, and equally important, to see those who are already part of the Kingdom community. "No one gets left behind," means the recovery of twenty-twenty, three hundred sixty degree vision.

Our inability to see this way has resulted in two crippling dysfunctions.

First, is our tendency to dismiss those we know in the Christian community at the cost of our distinct witness to the world. If, as Jesus said, our love for one another will be the gateway through which others will see the beauty of discipleship (John 13:35), then our inability to see each other well communicates just as loudly.

When someone new (to us) begins connecting to our faith community, we tend to be very accepting. We love that someone loves us, and so we see them through the rose-coloured glasses they generally see us through. Over time, familiarity reveals these people who have come our way as actually being very human. Suddenly they are among us as very wounded, needy, vulnerable, and unlovable people. Soon the initial shine is lost and we slide comfortably into the relational shallows. "How are you doing?" becomes merely a polite greeting that we expect to be answered with a smiling, generic "Fine." Anything beyond that takes us off guard and causes us to look for an opportunity to escape. People end up being hard work.

Furthermore, the arrival of a rabid new believer can unsettle the frozen chosen. Their blazing new faith can light unwelcome fires. Newborn babes are what we pray for, but when they're born they can reveal that we are unprepared caregivers. Their zealous presence may uncover deep-seated corporate dysfunction and spiritual apathy on our part that would rather not be challenged or brought to the light of day. Slowly, we abandon these new believers, too.

This dismissal applies all the more to those who have always been one of "us." We assume we know each other. We know, or think we know, where we stand on issues, so we avoid conversations that might lead to conflict. As a result, we lead superficial and shallow lives with those who are our brothers and sisters in Christ. Of course, like any family, when push comes to shove we tend to be there for one another. Still, is this truly the vision Jesus had in mind when he said "By this all people will know that you are my disciples, if you have love for one another"?

If we don't see ourselves as a beautifully diverse people, as sinners saved by grace, as vessels of the Holy Spirit, as pilgrims together on a journey, we will inevitably leave someone behind—and justify doing so. We begin elevating our agenda above Jesus' vision for his disciples. We believe it is our style of ministry or worship that communicates our discipleship to the watching world. In assuming this we are tragically wrong and compromise the one area people without Christ notice most—our uncommon ability to see one another as people and our selfless love for the saints and sinners alike.

Jesus is seen much more powerfully in our loving and serving embrace of one another than in the songs we sing or the programs we run. The greatest witnesses we have to offer those seeking hope and meaning is not our razzle and dazzle, but the loving embrace of our brothers and sisters. True family is incredibly attractive to orphaned souls. By leaving each other behind, we may be leaving more behind than we ever imagined.

Of course, the reason we leave others behind, even unintentionally, is that it is hard and often discouraging labour. Dietrich Bonhoeffer points out in his book *Life Together* that a breakthrough happens only when disappointment emerges from the frank recognition that we are not part of the ideal community, nor will we ever be. When the hard work of loving and enduring one another comes into view, we begin to see the flowering of God's intention for the new humanity. Bonhoeffer writes, "Only that fellowship which faces such disillusionment, with all its unhappy and ugly aspects, begins to be what it should be in God's sight, begins to grasp in faith that promise that is given to it."[1] In other words, to see people is to see them as they are, as Christ is in the process of transforming them, and loving them anyway.

Second, crippling dysfunction is a wrongful expectation of leaders. If we are still only seeing people from a human perspective—which Paul told the Corinthians is no longer what we do once we see Christ for who he is (2 Corinthians 5:16)—then we happily leave to a professional clergy the task of perceiving what the whole body must be awake to. Our current pattern of perceiving the Church results in our expectation that those who lead us will see people on behalf of the rest of us.

Within such a context we are soothed by having therapeutic professionals in our employ who see people's needs and respond in our stead. We pat ourselves on the back for the chaplaincy we are supporting. We celebrate that our ministers or pastors are doing God's work, but completely miss the fact that seeing people is a function of the Spirit's work in all of us and not the lonely calling of a priestly class. Consequently, seeing people becomes another program or specific professional vocation when it should primarily be viewed as a central value and vocation of the whole people of God—including children, youth, adults, and seniors. We will delve more deeply into this topic in a later chapter.

In such dysfunctional contexts, we begin to make excuses for leaving others behind. Here are a few you may have heard or even uttered yourself:

- I'm too busy.
- My show is on, so I'll do it later... if I remember.
- They *always* need help.
- I'm scared and don't know what to do or say.
- They never say thanks.

---

[1] Dietrich Bonhoeffer, *Life Together*, 27.

NO ONE GETS LEFT BEHIND

- I am uncomfortable around people like that.
- It will cost too much time, energy, and probably money.
- I'm still too busy.
- They had it coming.
- Someone else will do it.

Sounds so Jonah-like, does it not? When we respond this way, Josiah remains lost.

Over time, the fallout of this justified abandonment of people is an increasing blindness to them. Consequently, in relationships we can only be nice. "Nice" is an entirely unbiblical notion. "He was nice" is what the neighbours say to a reporter about the guy who just committed a heinous crime. "Nice" is a sign that we do not actually see people, but have instead dismissed them. Perhaps our deep conversation has only been, "Hey, how's it going?" We may be nice, but we have yet to see the person. Nice is a dismissive term; the jargon of non-relationship.

This pervasive "niceness" is especially subtle and destructive in the face of the postmodern tolerance that pervades western culture and which we are feverously exporting to the whole world. African theologian Emmanuel Katongole zeroes in on the troubling truth that there is "something sinister" about this postmodern world. Our blanket celebration of difference and the unquestioned championing of tolerance actually results in us "shielding ourselves from listening to or attending to the particular and historical claims of the 'other.'"[2] In other words, despite our apparent niceties and open-mindedness, we have no time and little care for each other's stories. We are nice strangers, indifferent and tolerant from a safe distance.

Culturally, then, we are told to see everyone as nice and to be nice, but this is really a sinister slippery slope toward taking no one in the least bit seriously. If we are only nice, we do not truly appreciate the other's uniqueness and potential blessing in my life. We just walk by with a shallow smile, wave, and nod. If we are only nice, we have yet to care for the wholeness and well-being of the other. If we are only nice,

---

[2] Emmanuel M. Katongole, *A Future for Africa*, 76.

we take no interest in the story that has shaped their beauty, pain, and even ugliness. And, to our great shock, we discover that no one knows our story either. Nor does it seem they care. Our world is left to us desolate.

A culture of "Nice" is simply a sign that we have yet to see people and are leaving them behind. After all, everyone has a story and all our stories are a mix of tragedy, drama, and comedy. We are who we are because of our histories. A missional Kingdom culture will pay attention to those stories and deal kindly, Christly, and mercifully with all who are waging great battles. A missional Kingdom culture exudes Kingdom kindness, which after all is a fruit of the Spirit (Galatians 5:22). Genuine kindness is a radical and under-resourced commodity in this world because it is part of the nature of God.

This means, therefore, that our great desire for the people we see is that they know it is ultimately God, their Creator and Redeemer, who desires they not be left behind. The God of the Bible, as Hagar voiced, is the God who sees us (Genesis 16:13). The incarnation of Jesus is the supreme example of this reality. In his life and ministry, Jesus was constantly seeing people ignored and dismissed. Further, as Paul describes triumphantly, even while we were yet seen only in our sin, Christ died for us (Romans 5:8).

Our goal is for God's vision and will to be realized in lives. That will mean our Kingdom kindness embracing others with compassion and mercy, while at the same time speaking truth in love. It means we will labour for the restoration of righteousness in word, deed, and relationship. Too often we are happy and self-satisfied to see a person regularly in the pew on Sunday morning, but our pews are full of people with lonely and stunted discipleship because no one has ever truly *seen* them and invited or challenged them into a deeper life in Christ. To see people missionally, to leave no one behind, is to see and yearn for what can be when Jesus is fully alive in us, and thereby alive in our communities.

And so, the great vocation of those who name Christ Lord these days is very simple: begin looking over your shoulder.

God is constantly looking over his shoulder for those who are falling behind, running away, or even mocking the flock. The Old Testament law included the simple command to leave some grain in the fields each harvest season for foreigners and the poor (Leviticus 19:9-10). God notices people easily overlooked. He sees something in the childless couple, Abram and Sarai. He notices something in Jacob, that jerk of a twin. He perceives hope in a spoiled brat and despised brother named Joseph. Moses the fugitive, David the runt of the litter, Ruth the foreign widow, and Esther the orphan are all examples of the divine joy in seeing what human eyes can't or won't see.

Jesus also embodies this vision-ability. Who really would have seen in his motley crew the potential to change the world? Peter, Matthew, Thomas... what would you have seen in them? Jesus sees the blind man everyone else has tuned out (Mark 10). He sees the haemorrhaging woman everyone else would shun (Mark 5). He looks up to see Zacchaeus on his perch and invites himself for supper when everyone else sees only an unpatriotic sell-out and royal pain in the bottom line (Luke 19). He sees the not-so-hidden life of a woman at a well in the heat of the day (John 4) and he sees children whom even his disciples would rather not have barging in on the serious life of big people (Mark 10). Jesus sees. In fact, it could be argued that the radical cultural and global revolution initiated by Jesus was grounded in his sight as much as his speech. What he said seemed to carry more weight because of what he saw in people—the good, the bad, and the ugly.

To join God in mission, therefore, must include this passion to leave no one behind. A missional Kingdom culture will see people with staggering possibilities where others only see trouble, mess, and imperfection. It will mean finding ourselves in places and with people we never dreamed possible, or even proper. It will mean knowing much more fully what it means to be the salt and the light of the world (Matthew 5:13-14). It will mean having to live with a more confident trust in the Spirit's work in our own lives and communities. It will require the strength and courage to be different, to engage and embrace others differently because our sight has been restored. It will mean setting aside our rights for others. It will mean trading indifferent tolerance for compassionate, engaged kindness. It will mean living with an uncompromising vision for the world as God sees it. It will mean having the attitude of Jesus (Philippians 2:5-11).

Holy vision is abnormal, and so we are an abnormal people with above average sight. After all, what will happen to the Josiahs and Ninevehs surrounding us if we who are seen and known by Jesus will not live this way?

UPON FURTHER REVIEW...

- What would you be doing differently as an individual or congregation if your guiding principle was "What will happen to the people?"
- Has there been a time when disappointment with your local church family actually became the avenue for a deeper seeing of others and a new love among God's people?
- Who are the people just over your shoulder these days not being embraced or kindly engaged?

A KINGDOM CULTURE THAT
EMBRACES AND ENGAGES MESS

For God so loved the world...

JESUS (JOHN 3:16)

...I know there is a God because in Rwanda I shook hands with the devil. I have seen him, I have smelled him and I have touched him. I know the devil exists, and therefore I know there is a God.

LIEUTENANT GENERAL ROMEO DALLAIRE
U.N. FORCES COMMANDER IN RWANDA (1993-1994)

One of the most influential people in my life was an adulterer. In my mid-twenties, I came to know, superficially in hindsight, a man named Dominic.[3] Dominic and I became friends. We met regularly for lunches, breakfasts, and afternoon and late night coffee chats, even though I didn't drink coffee.

His story was full of woe. His parents divorced when he was young and even as an adult he sought the missing approval and blessing of his father. He had made some bad decisions along the way and got hooked by wrong addictions and habits. On the flip side, he was a stunningly gifted athlete and craftsman and a hoot to be with. As well as I knew him, however, I still did not really *see* my friend.

One day, I picked up the phone to the sobs of his frantic wife on the other end of the line. She had just received a desperate message from a teenage girl claiming that her mother and Dominic were having an affair. There had been hints along the way that I should probably have paid more attention to, but I hadn't ever expected something of this magnitude. For three years, essentially as long as I had known him, Dominic had been cheating on his lovely wife and jeopardizing the future of his two kids. I was supremely ticked.

Two other men went with me to approach him and break the news that the jig was up. Now *he* got angry. He stomped out of the

---

[3] This is not his real name.

house, leaving his wife and the rest of us bewildered at the kitchen table. I didn't know if I would ever see him again. To be honest, I wasn't sure if I wanted to.

We had given him an ultimatum of sorts. If he changed course, we would be there for him with arms open. If he walked away, that was his choice, not ours. He chose to repent, and that choice was in many ways the path of *most* resistance. What his position of humility, or perhaps desperation, meant was that we—those two other guys and I—were committed to enter the mess of Dominic's life with a commitment to not leave him behind. The cost would be high. It would be even higher than first thought. It would have been much easier to refuse this painful embrace and let him go his way. I understand why the towel is so easy to throw in.

We persevered. We met with Dominic weekly, sometimes two or three times a week, for hours at a time, deconstructing his life with his invitation to find the truth, to heal the wounds, to find forgiveness and reconciliation. Months went by, taking one step forward and two steps back. Sometimes his hysterical phone calls would come in the middle of the night and I would find myself sitting beside him in the moon-light on a hard asphalt parking lot while he chain-smoked and drank yet another extra large java—which was better than the alternatives he could have drowned his sorrows in.

It was hard, really hard, to gauge growth and transformation. What benchmarks do you use to measure a journey back from the pit? How do you evaluate progress when you're cleaning up after a hurr-icane? Yet slowly, and ever so surely, Dominic began to demonstrate signs of new life. Forgiveness and grace took on a whole new meaning for each of us who were walking closely with him. He smiled more, smoked less, and began drinking decaf—a major accomplishment in and of itself. And, very significantly, he began to woo his wife again.

It was a long, tough, agonizing haul, but we trudged forward. About a year and half after the bomb dropped, we celebrated Dominic's move back home with his wife on Father's Day weekend. We were overjoyed, amazed, and awash in praise. It seemed enough battles had been won to declare the war over.

Half a year later, however, Dominic collapsed, in a coffee shop of all places. He was full of cancer. He was only in his early thirties. We were dismayed. Nevertheless, he tackled this new challenge with great faith and hope, supported by great love. He was ready to die because he had learned how to live, but he was ready to live because he had finally died to himself. A few months into his treatments, he and his wife renewed their vows before family and friends. What celebration! I can still see his satisfied, grateful, beaming smile as he sat exhausted from the day's festivities. The cancer treatments wore out his body, but not his spirit. His life had become a model for me.

Then, within a year, my friend died.

Even now, more than a half decade later, it's not uncommon for my heart to yearn for a chat about sports, politics, marriage, daddying, and Jesus over coffee and a donut with my friend. He taught me so much about life, about grace, about Jesus. He taught me how to forgive, ask for forgiveness, and be forgiven. He showed me how to persevere and live gratefully. And Dominic taught me that to leave no one behind requires the discipline of embracing and engaging mess.

In the everyday life of Kingsfield-Zurich Mennonite Church, our leadership team (spiritual overseeing body of elders) and pastoral care team (caring and nurturing body of deacons) meet occasionally to pray through the whole church family in one sitting. I introduce our prayer time with a warning: what we are about to do is bound to result in extra work for all of us called to lead this assembly of saints, because when we pray together—naming people, families, and situations—we are praying some people out of crisis and others into it.

When we seek God's will in the lives of those around us, it is sure to result in great rejoicing and equally great upheaval. Being serious about pursuing Christ-like transformation in lives is messy work. If we are not ready for a mess, we are not ready for transformation and we have yet to truly see people and understand what it is to be a missional Kingdom culture.

In the weeks following those intensive prayer gatherings, where each person, young and old, in our congregational sphere is prayed for by name, the proverbial manure inevitably hits the proverbial fan. Stuff begins to happen that taxes our wisdom, patience, resources, and courage and we are left to rely on God in new ways, realizing that we prayed for this. We pray for people by name because it is our determination to leave no one behind, yet that determination must be coupled with our commitment to accept the responsibility and privilege to embrace and engage the mess that the collision of light and darkness brings.

Far too often we expect the work of the Holy Spirit in people's lives will be simple. Just pray a prayer at an altar and a great spiritual awakening and transformation will be zapped into a life and caught like lightning in a bottle. Nice, tidy, and easy. Think again. I know my life, heart, and growth into Christ-likeness is not that simple, so why should I expect it to be true for others? A field that yields a great harvest requires both cultivation and fertilization long before any crop is produced. The harvest can be great fun, but fertilizer can stink to work with.

A brief survey of Jesus' power to transform people in the Gospels is revealing. Without a doubt, Jesus healed miraculously. He still does. Yet many of the lives he touched with wonders moved into new challenging seasons of life as a direct result of their encounter with the Anointed One. The once demon-possessed man of the Garasenes had some relational fences to mend with his neighbouring pig farmers. The whole community is more than a little unsettled about the whole miracle and ask Jesus to take the first boat out of town (Luke 8:26-39). It is really no surprise that the newly "delivered" man begged Jesus to take him away too. When one Sabbath day Jesus heals a man born blind, the political and social ramifications come into clear view (John 9). The receiver of the miracle becomes a target for interrogation and cross-examination. Even his parents are dragged into the mess. The point is that when we become accustomed to our messes, being delivered from them, having the transforming work of God burst upon us, is not all roses, cream cakes, and Kum Ba Yah.

With the children of Israel, we discover that leaving the wildernesses of our lives—even when led by the gentle hand of the Good Shepherd—is sometimes harder and messier than remaining a wanderer. Which is why, I suspect, we can be hesitant to pray. The earthquake of deliverance is unsettling. The price is high. Jesus comes proclaiming peace, but ends up bringing a sword that cuts a swath through our hearts, relationships, homes, and communities (Matthew 10:34-38). His reign does not allow for rivals. He moves in and everything else must go. When his Kingdom comes and his will is done on earth as it is in heaven, we begin to realize just how messy and hellish things can be.

As mentioned in the previous chapter, we readily welcome newcomers to our congregations with open arms, but often their sudden presence should raise red flags. I have learned that it is almost always the case that someone connecting "out of the blue" to a local church is doing so because life has become a clear and present danger and they are at the point of desperation. "Maybe God and those Christians can help," they may say to themselves. Their arrival is a visible demonstration of the cry of their hearts. This does not mean, of course, that we brand them with an "X" in super-indelible ink. It does mean that we who know Jesus must be awake to the reality that, if we are a people who are consistently demonstrating a culture where no one is left behind, we can expect messy lives to find us because we'll also be finding them.

But we might ponder: doesn't this openness say that we're really soft on the obedient and holy life of discipleship? Where does this culture of engaging and embracing messiness find biblical precedence?

First of all, it goes without saying that our great desire in leaving no one behind is for the righteousness of Christ to come alive in people made in God's image. We desire to see people walk in newness of life and in obedience to the commands of Jesus. His Truth sets people free. We are disciples making disciples. We cannot apathetically dismiss sin, nor can we sanction with tolerant blessing what a righteous and just God cannot stomach.

At the same time, too many churches have, in a determination to defend high moral ground, turned into courtrooms rather than maternity wards. We have judged lives based on outward appearance or current life-circumstance and not had eyes to see what is yet to be when Christ is named Lord and the Holy Spirit takes up residence. In many such churches, the pre-Jesus Matthew, Mary Magdalene, and

Zacchaeus would hardly find a welcome. To leave no one behind and walk with them on the path of life in Christ requires we step from our judge's benches and put on the gown and mask of an obstetrician. If we do this, we will gloriously catch some messy babies who will yet clean up and mature.

We all begin the life of discipleship in a mess. Sometimes it is only when we begin down the road in the footsteps of Jesus that the Spirit begins to reveal just how untidy things really are. When Jesus moves in, our invitation and the collision of the divine with our disorder leaves collateral damage. Hence, if we are truly a missional Kingdom culture, we ought to hope for more Dominics and prepare for some pretty heavy engagement with stuff we would rather not deal with. To leave no one behind, therefore, requires embracing the messiness of people because of the vision Jesus has for them while not being bound to our limited perspective and sawdust-infected eyes (Matthew 7:3).

Secondly, the entire Scriptures speak of God's willingness to embrace and engage the human mess. In fact, it is almost impossible to think of a biblical situation in which the Living Holy God does *not* humble himself to endure the mess of things on this planet for a greater purpose. We could think of Adam and Eve, Cain and Abel, Noah and his family, Hagar, Ruth, and David... to highlight just a few. Furthermore, let us think again of that profound verse which captures the whole, *"For God so loved the world, that he gave his only Son, that whoever believes in him should not perish but have eternal life"* (John 3:16).

God loved the world. The entire motivation for God's invasion of enemy territory[4] was love of a fallen, sin-scarred, warring, broken, indifferent, idolatrous, messy world. It was while we were yet his enemies that the Father sent the Son to reconcile us to himself and restore peace (Romans 5:1-8). The goal of this divine invasion was the movement of people, God's precious possession, from a life that is perishing into a life that is eternal. In sending the Christ, God essentially came to rescue his enemies from the losing side. This eternal life is not some "other side of the grave" escapism. Rather, it is a here and now and forevermore assurance of a Kingdom come on earth as it is and will be in heaven.

---

[4] This is C.S. Lewis' description of the incarnation in his book *Mere Christianity.*

21

Eternal life is to know the one true God who was sent (John 17:3). To know the one true God is to be rescued from the mess of a world lost in sin and to re-enter life with a new mission from a new King. We don a new set of clean armour (Ephesians 6:10-20) and live determined to leave no one behind on that stinking battlefield from which we all have been snatched. As Jesus was sent by the love of the Father into this world, so we who are saved by grace are sent (John 17:18).

Any sense of Eden-esque nostalgia we might naively have of this world ought to be laid to rest from the outset. This world has been an increasing mess from Adam and Eve's *un*fruitful snack and Cain's rubbing out of his brother to this very day. News headlines proclaim the never-ending cesspool of human depravity that can be both stomach-turning and strangely numbing. We have become a culture so conditioned by headline entertainment that our collective depravity no longer shocks us. Journalist Chris Hedges, who patrolled the Serbia-Kosovo chaos of the late 1990s, says, "We have nothing to fear from those who do or do not believe in God; we have much to fear from those who do not believe in sin."[5] The unique responsibility the church bears on behalf of the world is this unwelcome reminder: the mess lives within us all! Sin exists, we are sinners, and this sinful world is spinning out of control. This we must declare and lovingly and humbly confess. The Church has no excuse for not naming the mess what it is. Leaving no one behind means we cannot be indifferent about the disaster area we call home and our part in it.

Our fearful departure from a willingness to name sin and its symptoms, even within the Church these days, is a neon sign pointing to the loss of a missional Kingdom culture. We have somehow come to believe that soft-peddling the great disease we all share will make our message more palatable. Instead it has only made our message irrelevant and our programming a self-help abuser's paradise. Ironically, it is Hollywood and popular culture that remind us in a never-ending smorgasbord of ways that this world is a damned mess. Meanwhile Christians, who ought to be engaging what culture seems begging to have addressed, seem intent on declaring that it's really not that bad after all. It's time for the children of God to bravely confess

---

[5] Chris Hedges, *I Don't Believe in Atheists*, 13-14.

that we have not embraced and engaged as our God has, that this has blasphemed his holy name, and joyfully sing a new and courageous tune: this sinful world is a mess and we love it.

When Lieutenant General Dallaire found himself in the precarious place of leading an inept and hamstrung United Nations response to the 1994 genocide in Rwanda, he came face to face with the world God so loved. In his book recounting his traumatic experience, hauntingly titled *Shake Hands With the Devil*, Dallaire shares his hunch that the root of the careless response of the world's most powerful nations to the crisis in Rwanda was "fundamental indifference ... to the plight of seven to eight million black Africans in a tiny country that had no strategic or resource value to any world power." While 800,000 Rwandan men, women, children, and babies were being hacked to death, the world stood by watching the tragedy unfold on television, immunizing itself once more against the mess with that most conven-ient of technological advancements, the remote control. Dallaire describes how this indifference was summarized politically by a group of bureaucrats who arrived in Kigali to asses the situation in the early days of the genocide. They concluded, "We will recommend to our government not to intervene as the risks are high and *all that is here are humans*" (emphasis added).[6]

"All that is here are humans." If the Church ever needed a wake-up call to embrace and engage the mess we inhabit in order to leave no one behind, here it is in convicting black and white. The people who know God are keenly aware of what will happen to people both now and into eternity. As such, we will embrace the mess—even on both sides of the equation—in order to move a person, household, village, city, or nation to the eternal life that invades and infiltrates the world when God is known and people are seen.

"All that is here are humans." Yes, and they are messy. Yes, and to love them as God does will require an embrace and engagement with much of what we wish would not exist, and sometimes stupidly con-

---

[6] Romeo Dallaire, *Shake Hands With the Devil*, from the introduction.

clude does not. The world is a mess, but there ought to be at least one group of borderless people who will not be indifferent, and those people ought to be known as "Christians"—the followers of Jesus, the little Christs. We bear the name of the most embracing and engaging Presence in history. The day has dawned when we must embrace the messy adventure given to us, because everywhere we look people, human beings made in the image of God of every race, gender, age, class, and circumstance are being left behind.

Josiah is lost and must be found. Somebody must leave the comfort of the camp. Those in a missional Kingdom culture are eager to engage the mess and struggle of the wilderness because they know they've been found and their sight has been restored.

UPON FURTHER REVIEW...

- Discuss situations in which God led you, or your congregation, to step into the mess of the world with his love. What were the results?
- Are we prone to avoid the messy situations that surround us? Why is that? How can we become more courageous and risky? What might it cost us?
- How can the Church embrace and engage the messiness of our culture with the message of eternal life when the culture often interprets that Good News invitation as intrusion and intolerance?

FOR THE TOOLBOX

A t four points throughout this book you will come to a section like this that will provide practical tools to grow the missional Kingdom culture declarations in your context. I know how easy it is to skip over exercises like this. The value of this study, however, to you as an individual, team, or congregation, will only be enhanced as you take time to discuss, engage, and implement at least a few of these helpful resources.

As a case in point, let me share with you what happened when the elders of Kingsfield-Zurich Mennonite Church retreated together in the fall of 2006. Besides the fun, fellowship, food, and practical joking, we took time to work through Peter Scazzero's "Inventory of Spiritual/Emotional Maturity" (You'll learn more about this tool below).

Of the fifteen leaders gathered that weekend, eleven were raised in Mennonite homes. What emerged from the survey was the startling discovery that those of us raised in the Mennonite Christian tradition shared the identical areas of spiritual/emotional maturity *and* immaturity. Those not raised in Mennonite communities did not share these characteristics—they had other strengths and issues to add to the mix. Given that the majority of our church family at the time shared some form of Mennonite rooting, this opened our eyes as leaders and lent words to what was a general pattern in the broader congregation. In fact, it shed immediate light on why certain issues and problems continued to rear their ugly heads. The true issue, we recognized, was the need for a more whole spiritual maturity.

Coming home from the retreat, we determined as a team of leaders to celebrate more wildly the places of maturity among our people and work more vigorously at addressing the particular area of immaturity that we identified in ourselves. Since that weekend, in the autumn of 2006, we have, in a variety of ways, been able to grow our fellowship as a more mature and balanced people in Christ as a result of a very simple, yet helpful tool. It is this type of insight and healthy development that I pray can also become your experience.

There are, of course, a myriad of helpful tools available that can be utilized, both personally and corporately. Consider this to be more equipment to help with the necessary maintenance and tuning of a people on the Way.

In building a growing capacity to be a people who leave no one behind, the following corporate tools can be effective aids in the healthy development of your missional Kingdom culture:

a. **Rediscover Prayer**

Congregational Prayer Retreats: Dream and develop ways of corporately praying for one another, your church, your community, and your mission as a people. This should involve your key leaders and take significant time. Go beyond token prayers; name people individually and invite God's will be done in their homes and lives. Be prepared for messy situations to emerge. Create a culture that calls on God and waits upon the Spirit's work.

Walk-by-Prayer: Praying by walking the streets of your community is another powerful way to begin to "see" people in new ways. Every home has a story, often hidden, that only God sees. Walking (or driving) by the houses of your community with prayerful hearts can not only awaken a deeper compassion for your neighbours, but will begin to bear fruit in bringing to light the mess and pain of the world close to you.

Prayer Narratives: Another way to open your eyes is to name the narratives of sin and salvation in your church and community. Where does the newspaper or your local, national, and ethnic histories reveal patterns of sin that need to be named and prayed against? Likewise, recognizing similar patterns in the stories of God's saving work in your community can be equally transforming. This discipline can open your eyes to stories of redemption and where the Gospel is finding traction with the people of your sphere of influence. You might discover that your energies and resources have been focused in rather unfruitful places.

b. **The Emotionally Healthy Church**

This excellent book by Peter Scazzero *(The Emotionally Healthy Church: A Strategy for Discipleship that Actually Changes Lives)* has much to offer in aiding the formation of a missional Kingdom culture. Especially useful is the Inventory of Spiritual/Emotional Maturity (pages 59-65), as just referenced from our own church's experience. This tool opens windows of understanding of the relationship between the individual believer and the corporate body. It brings awareness to our healthy embrace of people or where we are leaving people behind because of spiritual immaturity that needs to named and acknowledged.

c. **Take road trips**

Road Trip Relationships: Get key leaders, committees, or small groups involved in ministry settings outside your church building, program, and fellowship. Take road trips to places where life is messy or to learn from organizations that are dealing with the realities of your community and society that are often invisible. Building relationships with people other than you (including non-Christians) who are seeking to serve your community can be transforming and enlightening. You might even consider the "rebellious" move of doing some of this road-tripping on a Sunday morning to really shake loose the missional cobwebs.

Outer Spaces: Having ministry teams do their work and planning in different spaces—like a coffee shop, park, or local restaurant—can help them remember why they're doing what they're doing. This can awaken new conversation and release new vision. It is actually the practicing of missional ministry in seed form. It also communicates to those who see the church in this visible form that the people of God are truly "for" this community and unashamed of their identity as people who follow Jesus.

Statistically Speaking: It is possible to take enlightening "road trips" of your area through demographic studies. Using census data and local or national government statistics can paint a surprising picture of the people in your area that you don't want to leave behind. It can also help provide a clearer picture of the type of people your church is most likely to connect with and where you need to grow in crossing cultural barriers that we might be blind to.

CHAPTER TWO

"Our Leaders Lead"

Let the Kingdom Come...

New College at Oxford is not really new at all. Originally founded in 1379 by William of Wykeham, Bishop of Winchester, it was the first undergraduate college at Oxford.

The Black Death had spread from Asia to Europe by the late 1340s, and by the end of 1350 Europe had lost nearly half its population to the sweeping pandemic. England was hit especially hard, with whole parts of cities and country villages left emptied. The toll on pastors was especially grim. Giving care to the sick and officiating endless funerals constantly exposed them to the disease. It was not long before there was a desperate shortage of properly educated church leaders throughout England.

Bishop William recognized the dilemma facing the communities of his charge, so he proposed the development of a new training centre to fill the leadership vacuum. William was active in both spiritual and political spheres and had the ear of King Richard II. New College was his solution to the problem of uncovering and developing youth of humble origins who could serve as spiritual leaders in desperate times. The King allowed the college's construction to proceed uninhibited, and so the New College of St. Mary (so named because there was already another school dedicated to Mary) was raised on the northeast corner of the Oxford city walls—an area that had a sordid reputation as the city's red light district and dumping ground for everything your Mom tells you to run from like the plague. What a great place to train pastors!

William of Wykeham's college was new for other reasons as well. The college's motto, developed by the bishop, was "Manners Makyth Man." While our postmodern minds might snicker at such a slogan, William was actually well ahead of his time. Firstly, he had the foresight to write the motto in English rather than Latin, over a hundred years before William Tyndale would be born. Tyndale was eventually burnt at the stake for translating the Scriptures into English. Secondly, his caption says, in an age where patronage and lineage meant everything, that a person is not defined by blood lines, money, or property, but by how they behave towards other people. In other words, it's who we are and how we live, not what we have, that matters most. "Manners Makyth Man" was a radical counter-cultural vision statement.

Another "new" development of the college was its layout and architectural design. It became the first college at Oxford to centre on a main quadrangle, a court-yard completely surrounded by student rooms, a dining hall, library, study spaces, great hall, and of course chapel. Such a blueprint meant a New College student's life would be focused entirely on the life of the college, with everything they needed provided within the unity of this one location. At its opening, New College boasted the grandest collection of buildings among any of the Oxford colleges. It became a highly respected school, eventually prompting King Henry VI to create King's College at Cambridge in its mould.

Over the next few centuries, the College went through highs and lows, reaching perhaps one of its most critical periods in the mid 1800s. In 1850, there were only a handful of undergraduate students enrolled. The quality of education and develop-ment envisioned by the good Bishop was in shambles. Furthermore, the grounds and buildings were in equally poor repair. Five hundred years after being raised, the great beams supporting the roof of the great hall and chapel were rotted through.

Aware that her future hung in the balance, and inspired by her sister college at Oxford, the reform-minded Balliol, New College dared to imagine a different world. The great Victorian and Gothic architect Sir George Gilbert Scott was hired to restore the roof of the hall and chapel, the school's symbolic heart. So it was that Sir Scott and representatives from the college took a trip together to the Great Hall Woods of Berkshire, hoping to find trees for replacement beams—not just any regular lumber would do. Sure enough, the replacements were standing there, waiting

to be hewn out of the now fully-developed trees that had been planted by some
visionary and anonymous soul a century earlier for just that very purpose.[7]

So many aspects of this short re-telling of New College's history
provide the perfect introductory parable for our desire to live out a
missional Kingdom culture that says, "Our leaders lead."

First of all, Bishop William responded to the cultural challenges of
his day, many outside of his control, a culture reeling with grief and
pain, with startling vision and courage. Depleted leadership resources
in a dark night of fear and death did not stop a new vision for what
could be, but rather seemed to inspire one. In a day when it would have
been easy to shrink back, give up, dream small, or go cheap, New
College actually seemed to embody a hope-filled vision despite the
hopelessness of the times. In addition, William's determination to
speak the emerging language of his English culture and chart a new
course for what gave worth to people says much about the man and his
understanding of the marks of true Christian leadership.

Furthermore, and this is particularly important to open our minds
to as we dig deeper into our second missional declaration, there was
some unknown bloke in Berkshire who made a fresh day for New
College possible. Someone with incredible foresight had performed the
simple, anonymous, yet essential task of planting saplings with a vision
for what they could one day become. Most likely they never lived to see
the fruit of their labour of love. Who, I wonder, is doing the literal and
metaphorical planting of small things that will need to be harvested in
2150?

---

[7] I am indebted to the website of New College, University of Oxford (www.new.ox.ac.uk),
Wikipedia, and Max DePree's *Leaderhip Jazz* for the piecing together of this story.

A KINGDOM CULTURE THAT VALUES VISION

O Jerusalem, Jerusalem, the city that kills the prophets and stones those who are sent to it! How often would I have gathered your children together as a hen gathers her brood under her wings, and you would not! See, your house is left to you desolate.

JESUS (MATTHEW 23:37-38)

I can abandon it or I can continue it as long as life goes on, or until the calf breaks its neck butting the oak, or until the oak cracks and comes crashing down.

ALEKSANDR I. SOLZHENITSYN

There are days I would rather mow lawns. For several summers, when my ministry only partially supported my family, I mowed lawns alongside my father-in-law. Rain or shine, I looked so forward to those days. No telephones and no complaints, unless I clipped a flower not intended for trimming, to which I could always say, "It'll grow back." There was plenty of time to think, pray, dream, and sing to the ongoing hum of that John Deere riding lawn tractor.

Since then, I have moved into positions where my ministry role pays full salary. This frees me to invest my energy in what I am passionate about, but can leave me coming home some days saying to my wife, "I wish I could just mow lawns."

Working with people is hard work. Working to implement a vision of life, community, and ministry effectiveness that understands the times and always asks "What will happen to the people?" is tedious and frequently misunderstood labour. It is, as Soviet dissident writer Aleksandr Solzhenitsyn so aptly describes, like a calf butting its head against an oak. To lead requires a stubborn streak, and some might say a masochistic tendency to constantly run your head up against that which seems immovable, while holding on to the slightest hope that eventually the mighty oak that has served its purpose may fall and make room for new life.

J. Oswald Sanders once wrote, "Often the crowd does not recognize a leader until he has gone, and then they build a monument for him with the stones they threw at him in life." Most living leaders have felt those stones. Most dead ones never got the monument, even posthumously. And when the pile of stones *is* raised in honour, it is only seen by the leader's progeny. Sometimes we don't know what we've got till it's gone.

In the movie version of Alexander the Great's life, one of Alexander's comrades grumbles, "The dreamers exhaust us; they must die before they kill us with their blasted dreams." It sounds so much like Joseph's brothers, who conspire to rid themselves of their obnoxious, irritating brother. *"Here comes this dreamer. Come now, let us kill him and throw him into one of the pits ... and we will see what will become of his dreams"* (Genesis 37:19-20). To be given a dream, to be saddled with a vision, to bear this burden for people, often means becoming public enemy number one.

Sadly, such a culture all too often exists within our churches. Every church, regardless of tradition, confession, or model, calls out and identifies leaders. We give them various titles or non-titles and ask them to meet together and model the way. We financially support some and expect others to volunteer. We expect them to build, understand, guide, and mind the ship. We expect them to move us along. We hope they will courageously protect us from wolves. We ask them to solve our problems and think through our complexities. We give them, in one way or another, a place of honour in our eyes and hearts, and maybe even our prayers, then proceed to neuter and hamstring them. We begin to pester them with the schizophrenic complaints the redeemed slaves of Israel heaped upon Moses: "Take us back to Egypt." "Lead us out, let's go back." "Tell us where to go, but not that way." We have a theology and ecclesiology acknowledging that God's economy includes gifts of leadership and the need for apostles, prophets, evangelists, pastors, and teachers. Too often, however, we call them out only to proceed to doubt the Spirit's wisdom and cry to have the cart lead the horse.

Even more disturbing is the full frontal attack on those who lead. The Apostle Paul had to defend himself to the Corinthians—a church he sacrificed much for. The Corinthians now dismiss him mockingly, *"His letters are weighty and strong, but his bodily presence is weak and his speech of no account"* (2 Corinthians 10:10). If the vision of the leader does not fit our fancy, or challenges our apathy, or rocks our boat, we begin a new strategy that is bound to work: discredit character, slam gifting, gossip about, and allow subtle innuendos to do their dastardly work. We excuse our own fragile humanity, ignoring our own unbiblical motives and means. We expect the leader to be Superman or Superwoman—then actively conspire to prove they are not. Inevitably we contradict the very words of Scripture, *"Obey your leaders and submit to them, for they are keeping watch over your souls, as those who will have to give an account. Let them do this with joy and not with groaning, for that would be of no advantage to you"* (Hebrews 13:17).

Most leaders I know would willingly, and sometimes even happily, endure these types of personal attacks if the vision birthed by God would at least be embraced or even endured. Kill the messenger, fine, but at least hear the message. With their Lord they cry out over the cities, towns, and side roads they are burdened with, "O Jerusalem, Jerusalem." They ache for right-living and Christlikeness to infuse lives, homes, marriages, work places, and schools. They are constantly concerned about what is happening to the people. They genuinely mourn the sin and brokenness they see around them. They are keenly aware of the darkness that lives within, reminding them to live a repentant life. And they bear this all because of the vision.

A genuine spiritual vision, a genuine picture of a better, more God-centered future is something only God can give. People do not create vision, God does. The promise, through the prophet Joel, is that when the Spirit is poured out, dreams and visions will be a present reality for God's people (Joel 2:28-29). Such visions are a Spirit-birthed grace, not a human-concocted plan. You can tell the difference between the two with just a little time in the Holy Writ and a dash of wisdom mixed with discernment.

When you get right down to it, a purely human vision will primarily be about prestige, pride, tradition, and personal advancement. It will be said to be possible, and in the words of Bob the Builder, "Yes, we can!" God, to a human vision, is an accessory, a mere chattel. A purely human vision will be driven at the expense of people, sometimes leaving them behind intentionally. It will need to be sold via yells and lies and will bring out the most depraved qualities of human nature— even if they are only seen behind closed doors. Some people are willing to die for a purely human vision, but even that death will have anger, malice, and superiority marked over the gravesite.

A genuine spiritual vision, on the other hand, will always make sense with what the Spirit has breathed in Scripture. It may not necessarily make sense from a human perspective. Most likely it will actually make no sense at all. Instead, it will stretch us beyond belief, but it will find a growing circle of settled "yeses" in the spirits of those who know Christ and truly seek God's will to be done on earth as it is in heaven. This spiritual vision will also tend to be carried by someone who is suffering greatly (even if that suffering is relatively unseen) for a cause they did not find, but that found them. A vision from God goes with the flow of Scripture, against the stream of God-less culture, and finds one lonely soul, or at best a motley remnant willing to be its ambassadors and champions.

When John the Baptist sits imprisoned near the end of his life, he begins to doubt the vision he had been given and spent his life proclaiming. Increasingly confused and battered by doubt, he sends word by his disciples to Jesus asking, *"Are you the one who is to come, or shall we look for another?"* Jesus' response is quite telling, *"Go and tell John what you hear and see: the blind receive their sight and the lame walk, lepers are cleansed and the deaf hear, and the dead are raised up, and the poor have good news preached to them. And blessed is the one who is not offended by me"* (Matthew 11:3-6). In essence, Jesus was reminding John to look carefully and judge whether Jesus' actions were in line with the vision God had already outlined in history. This is a vision that John himself had been a prophet of. Jesus was the vision of God in flesh, in living colour. Did he now offend? Will we once again despise the dreamer? If not, the freedom is there to celebrate that the vision of God for a sin-stained and diseased world is coming more and more into focus and rejoice that we have the opportunity to get on board.

Generally, our offence at vision is related to our own, or congregational, culture of fear and tendency toward idolatry. We fear losing what we know, even if we know that what we know is not what we wish we would know. We fear the unknown. Having spent so much time navel-gazing and locked in our prison, like John, we have ceased to appreciate God's vision being born and carried among us, and even the role we have had in revealing it thus far. Furthermore, our attachment to what is comfortable and known very easily and subtly slips into idolatry. We begin to worship our forms. The way it has always been done is raucously defended. We practically believe it is God, and not we, who must change.

As a result, the vision-bearers among us become suspect. They are suspiciously seen as instigators of doubt as to what we have thus far believed to be true. The dreamers are threats to our sad existence that we fear might change. What we fail to ask in the midst of our self-induced unspiritual noxiousness is whether or not this vision is another example of God's vision for humanity, described in Scripture about to be contextualized for a new day. If it is, we are the losers and to be pitied if we fail to take faithful steps in God's direction.

The leaders of this charge forward against the gates of hell also have a challenge set before them as vision-bearers and casters. They must stubbornly refuse the appeal to succumb to the temptation and comfort of pleasing people. Truth be told, most leaders will at one time abandon or put on the shelf a vision of great unction because they fear what it might bring them or cause them to lose. You may lose some friends, comfort, stability, sleep, and applause to bespeak and become the vision. To incarnate the vision of God is to put your foot in with the prophets stoned in Jerusalem, which is not exactly a strong incentive or retirement plan. Dietrich Bonhoeffer reminded the German leaders shortly after Hitler's rise to power in the 1930s, "Those who are still afraid of men have no fear of God, and those who have fear of God have ceased to be afraid of men. All preachers of the gospel will do well to recollect this saying daily."

Consequently, leaders must move forward in the fear of the Lord, ready to embody a vision that no one else may ever see, simply because it is the vision that found them. The leader must, of course, test the vision by Scripture and with the spiritual community, but at the end of the day he or she may end up bearing it alone for a long time before the vision becomes reality. As King Lune says to his heir Cor in C.S. Lewis' *The Horse and His Boy*, "For this is what it means to be king: to be first in every desperate attack and last in every desperate retreat, and when there's hunger in the land (as must be now and then in bad years) to wear finer clothes and laugh louder over a scantier meal than any man in your land." Leaders live, laugh, and die for what God says must be while remembering that the vision belongs to God and begins and ends with him.

This valuing of vision, which frees our leaders to lead us and not simply pander to us, is the task of the whole community, of the whole of God's people. The leader—and there are various leaders the church calls out, not just paid leaders—accepts the call of the Holy Spirit through the people of God. Likewise, the body of believers accepts the peculiar presence of one who will now, by that same Spirit, declare to us that our life as pilgrims is far from over and that this is no time to stop pressing on. The leader reminds the body of believers that this is no time to build with bricks and mortar, as though we had reached the end of our sojourn. Instead, the visionary rouses us to pack up our tents for the nomadic journey that is ours as foreigners and strangers in this world. The leader sounds the trumpet when the pillar of fire or cloud moves on. It is, after all, our transformed presence, our living out of God's vision for people and the world, that is our vocation together. We are a peculiar people just passing through and the valuing of vision keeps this peculiarity an accepted part of our identity.

When declaring our missional Kingdom culture, we say "Our leaders lead." By saying this, we are reminding ourselves that we are a community that values vision. It is not simply, however, that we value a new set of ideas or smile approvingly as we endure the wild dreams of those among us who seem to see another world and occasionally appear to be living there. No. The valuing of vision is much more beautiful than that. It is that we actually value attempted implementation of better ways and realities. We hope together for the realization of what is dreamed, but not yet seen. This corporate discipline provides tangible evidence that we really do walk by faith. Every new vision is proof of a world not seen or made by human hands.

Vision is proof that there is a heaven. Vision is a window into the eternal.

We live with a corporate restlessness with the way things are. No matter how good it may seem, we have not yet fully realized the Kingdom Jesus came proclaiming and initiating. We hold with grateful open hands what has already been done and refuse the temptation to declare finished the work of the Spirit in, among, and through us. We value and celebrate our history and heritage, but realize we cannot and do not live there anymore, neither do we long to.

A missional Kingdom culture takes the risk that a new vision of things not only can but must become our lived reality. God is constantly making all things new and bringing everything bit by bit, day by day, generation by generation under Christ—we ought to be his partners in these new advances. In the end, we realize that for all this to take place we must say "Our leaders lead!" and release them to dream, vision, shape the culture, and create systems among us by which our Spirit-filled missional impulse can take root and grow.

But how does this valuing of vision take root?

Practically speaking, to value vision and champion its implementation requires some basic corporate commitments:

First, a celebration of gifting. This will be addressed more fully later on, but at this point we must recognize that where there is no appreciation and celebration of the various gifts, personalities, dreamers, and even slow-on-the-uptake ones among us, we will not value vision well. Apart from the celebration of gifts God gives his people, we will miss the full implementation of God's vision for our times. We will miss asking the right questions and will not have the right people in the right places. If we are all expected to be the same, we will be planting seeds of conflict and division rather than missional unity and vision. Consequently, this celebration of gifting will require us to accept that those with vision and leadership ability among us (which aren't always the same thing) must be freed to bring their gift to the rest of the body—a move that will, in the long run, be cause for great and yet unseen celebrations. It is true that dreamers and visionaries disturb the peace, but that is precisely their gift to us. We would be wise to receive them with both endurance and thanksgiving.

Second, a celebration of change. A church culture that believes it has reached some paradise plateau of institutional Shangri-La has just reached it zenith and will shortly begin to die. Most great world empires built their greatest edifices and temples near the end of their reign of influence. Oh, the perception of health and vitality will remain, maybe for some time, but the first nail has gone in the coffin and only God will resurrect her. In these days of rapid, almost incalculable cultural change, the Church must be so grounded in the Truth handed down through the ages that spontaneous and effective change can be well rooted, quickly initiated, and even anticipated. It is Jesus Christ who remains the same, not our methods, models, or programs (Hebrews 13:8).

We ought to happily hold our forms with open hands so that they can be celebrated and set aside with joy because we realize the witness of the body of Christ in the world supersedes our comfort and sense of having arrived. We celebrate that the Church is an organism of constant growth, change, and transition more than an organization intended to foster stagnant bureaucracy.

Most church families celebrate baptisms, the birth and dedication of children, weddings, and other natural life transitions, but staunchly dig in their heals when it comes to the natural corporate transitions that take place over time within a body of living, breathing people who live in a constantly changing world. This, tragically, is often present in ridiculous battle-royals over music styles or the format of some outdated and over-tired programs or ministries. These battles are really symptoms of a deeper dysfunction that has beset a people unable to appreciate the seasons, recognize the times, and know what a people should do.

One of the first steps that can be taken to counter this debilitating and destructive force is to read the Scriptures again, to note the enormous changes that God has led his people through in the past, name what truly does stay the same, and then retell the stories of great changes that have been part of our own histories, personal and corporate. And then we should have the courage to submit ourselves to a very exposing question, "If we never did it this way before, is this the way we would devise it from scratch?" A commitment to celebrate change would be very open to honest and transforming answers to that question. A commitment to celebrate change will encourage a culture in which future generations are free to ask the same questions of our own implementing visions which will someday probably outgrow their nimbleness and fitness.

Third, a celebration of process. This commitment is very hard for me personally. I am one of those quick to initiate and embrace change (not necessarily in that order), and can therefore be a little dangerous—especially if I don't celebrate process. Process sounds like the evil twin to change, but in fact it is her perfect dance partner. Clear, deliberate, yet forward moving processes, that involve more and more saints, allow for the ongoing clarification and shared ownership of the vision God is giving to his people. It leaves room for a loyal opposition, will empower people to contribute their own voice and strengths, and ironically enough will become the avenue through which the vision is passionately defended and hard hearts challenged by people other than the vision-bearer.

This does not imply that we seek to silence an opposing view. The loyal opposition can be a vision's best friend by provoking thought, soul-searching, biblical investigation, and the asking of good questions. At the same time, however, we also need to expose and set aside cynicism, callousness, and criticism that is not of the Spirit of Jesus, but rather a subversive foothold of the devil. The correction of this destructive spirit is most corporately powerful when it comes from a wider diversity of the body and not solely from a leader or committee that can be accused of having a hidden agenda or thirst for power. In the end, we realize our battle is not against others who share our flesh and blood, and especially those who are brothers and sisters in Christ, and so we celebrate the process by which the vision of God for the transformation of a people is discerned, embraced, and brought into full bloom.

It must be noted, however, that process is not an endless cycle of meetings, discernment, excruciating tardiness, and ultimately frustrating indecision all in the name of keeping the peace. When it has been two years and we are still circling the same wagons, or the wagons are just plain stuck in a rut, the time has come to move on. Process can be very short and still done well, while at other times—depending on the nature of the vision—process must be more patient and inclusive. When we say "Our leaders lead" we are acknowledging that when process is done well, good decisions are made in the right way, by the right people. We release those God has called to oversee the flock to lead us to make visionary decisions so that the Kingdom truly advances as God intends. Wandering in the wilderness has never been a badge of honour for the people of God.

There is that tenuous and tender moment when the harvest is ripe. We need to be a people of process who know when the time to turn vision into tangible rubber-meets-the-road action has come. A missional Kingdom culture ultimately refuses to allow talk and endless meetings to become cheap religious entertainment with no obedient follow through. As Victor Hugo inspired, "There is one thing stronger than all the armies in the world; and that is, an idea whose time has come." It was, after all, following a season of process and preparation that the fullness of time came and God sent his Son (Galatians 4:4).

Fourth, a celebration of big dreams and small successes. I have a son who ends most days postponing sleep by talking up the big dreams that he has of building a motorbike from scratch or inventing some device out of scrap metal, pipe cleaners, empty cereal boxes, and duct tape that would change the course of human history. There are people in our congregations with equally eyebrow raising visions for what a God-inspired future could hold. Sometimes it sounds to the rest of us like so much nonsense. We equate it with the bedtime ramblings of a sleep-deprived child.

Hold the phone. That big dream may truly change the world, or even just one life. That big dream may be the spark needed to inspire some great new direction for the local church and beyond. We must celebrate the big dreams and hear them out, be they ever so far-fetched. Ever heard of Noah? When God births something, it is bound to be bigger than we have yet imagined and require more faith than we have yet mustered. Furthermore, God is likely to reveal it first to someone with a holy imagination that we had better make room in the inn for. Every St. Patrick, Conrad Grebel, William Wilberforce, Gladys Aylward, and Fanny Crosby came from somewhere.

Furthermore, this celebration of big dreams will mean the statement "We've never done it this way before" will actually be a positive and not paralyzing point. There ought to be a holy originality to a genuine spiritual vision birthed within the context of the age and locale in which we serve. The unending presence of big box and big name franchising we see in our cities and towns causes us to believe that we have only really arrived when a McDonald's or Wal-Mart blesses us with their consumerist presence. This false sense of identity also reveals itself in our churches when we carbon copy an original vision of contextualizing the dreams of God in some other place into our own body life because "everyone is doing it." While our eyes and hearts should be open to learn and be inspired by God's action elsewhere, the reality is that the Spirit that is creatively causing young and old to have vision "over there" is also seeking to birth the same right here. The celebration of big dreams will provide a wild space for the creativity of the Spirit to interpret the apostolic message in new ways for a new day in new places.

At the same time, it is equally important to celebrate the small success. Often God-inspired big vision becomes realized in bite-sized samplings before it becomes the full-course meal. Genuine spiritual vision in Scripture was often a long time in the making. It is imperative that we rejoice when and where vision is observed, even in seed form. It will be small mustard seeds that become the unbelievable foliage in which beautiful birds perch. It should be expected that the vision of God's future among us will first be witnessed in the micro before it becomes the macro and meta-narrative that defines the life and witness of the community in the next season of ministry.

Fifth, a celebration of anonymous tree planters. Someone had the foresight to plant the saplings of Great Hall Woods a century before New College realized they were needed. There are always current needs among us that anonymous and unseen souls walking close enough with the Lord years before were able to discern. Most likely, they were thought a little off their rocker by the realists of their day. Probably they had no idea of the full impact of their obedience. Aren't we grateful for them now? It's never too late to celebrate obedience to a vision given by God that may not have made sense at the time. The truth is, by faith we believe that in some mysterious way our strange obedience to the bizarre vision God births in us today may actually be meant to bear fruit well after we have become an anonymous reference in someone else's story. People in a missional Kingdom culture revel in the privilege of being listed as unknown soldiers. It is, after all, a clearer vision of our Lord we desire seen in increasing measure for generations to come.

Perhaps upon the return of his disciples with Jesus' vision-correcting answer to his vision-challenged question, John the Baptist recalled his own words, *"He must increase, but I must decrease"* (John 3:30). Now, there is a grand vision for our leaders to lead us toward, if we will let them. Sometimes the oak that the calf must keep charging is us.

UPON FURTHER REVIEW...

- Can you think of a vision God birthed in you (individually or corporately) that resulted in great fruit and surprising celebration? Can you think of a vision that was shelved, which in hindsight should not have been?
- Can you name any big dreams that should probably be taken more seriously? Can you point out some small successes that point to the realization of the vision God has for you?
- Who are the anonymous tree planters, or William of Wykeham visionary leaders, who need celebrating in your story?

A Kingdom Culture That Equips Saints

> *And he gave the apostles, the prophets, the evangelists, the pastors and teachers, to equip the saints for the work of ministry, for building up of the body of Christ...*
>
> The Apostle Paul (Ephesians 4:11-12)

> *When the work of the best rulers is done, their task accomplished, the people remark, "We have done it ourselves."*
>
> Laotse

At this point in my far from illustrious career as a troubadour of the King, I have served in three different pastoral leadership positions and one college deanship. One common thread has run through these leadership experiences that I have been privileged to serve: in each case, I replaced someone with a gift mix that was the polar opposite of mine. At one point, I thought this meant I was something special, but now I am beginning to wonder if I am merely the leadership medication for a corporate mental illness.

It took me a while to recognize and admit my strengths, because I was raised in a Mennonite tradition that frowned upon any personal recognition of ability and gifting. Somehow I picked up along the way that such self-awareness might lead to pride and arrogance, which would offend the Lord's fragile superiority complex and cause lightning to strike the real estate I stood on. So I learned to disregard my gifting, shrug off compliments with "Oh, it's nothing," never considering that to speak in such flippant and embarrassed terms about the Spirit's work in me was heinous pride turned upside down and outside-in. My so-called humility was as much a disregard for God's blessings as any of the boasting I may have been tempted to engage in. What I have come to admit—with fear and trembling—is that my particular strengths and gifts as a Spirit-filled disciple are both unique and necessary, but they are not ultimately *for* me.

In the movie version of J.R.R. Tolkien's grand epic, *The Lord of the Rings: The Return of the King,* Aragorn, the heir to the throne, finds himself face to face with the Elf Lord Elrond. Aragorn has been brave and demonstrated exemplary leadership in the struggle to unseat evil, but has been consistently hesitant to embrace his true calling as King. Into this timidity Elrond steps, and says to the royal son, "Lay aside the Ranger and be what you were meant to be." And he does. Tolkien's tale culminates with Aragorn crowned King with this epitaph over his reign:

> *In his time the City was made more fair than it had ever been, even in the days of its first glory; and it was filled with trees and fountains, and its gates were wrought of mithril and steel, and its streets were paved with white marble; and the Folk of the Mountain laboured in it, and the Folk of the Wood rejoiced to come there; and all was healed and made good, and the houses were filled with men and women and the laughter of children...*[8]

This sounds like the faithful and glorious reign of a benevolent and wise ruler. But what I am reminded of is that Aragorn, the King, needed to be called to the task prepared for him. Furthermore, the triumph of his leadership was the good of the people and the establishing of a glorious place to live, serve, and thrive. He was a King *for* something, not *of* something. Aragorn leads a mature, blessed, and blessing people. Of course, Aragorn is a fictional leader, but since truth can be stranger than fiction, perhaps fiction can shed light on the strange place we find ourselves.

There are strange ideas and assumptions around about what constit-utes leadership in the Christian community these days. Local churches, much like the culture at large, are suffering from a dearth of genuine leadership and a corruption of its nature and task.

To begin, we have a rather odd understanding of what and who a leader is. The administrative assistant in our office remarked recently at how "regular" and "normal" we were as a team of pastors. She meant

---

[8] J.R.R. Tolkien, *The Lord of the Rings: The Return of the King*, 297.

it as a compliment, for we had upended the assumptions about church leader types she had had before coming more closely into our daily circle. Leaders are too often believed to be individuals with spotless lives, lofty titles, higher educations, and the responsibility for keeping us feeling comfortable. This is a misunderstanding. While character is crucial and training is a worthwhile and necessary enterprise, an over-emphasis on human benchmarks for leadership ability can become a shaky foundation upon which to build a vibrant, mature missional Kingdom culture.

Where this misunderstanding persists, leadership is corrupted into the narrow confines of the professional spiritual elite, making it inaccessible and unbiblical. In many regards, this corruption was a root cause of the reformation and radical reformation[9] of the sixteenth century. Frustration with a religious vocational elite who had all the necessary human titles and had demonstrated a form of godliness whilst denying its power erupted in a radical renewal movement of the Holy Spirit that caused commoners, and not just diviners (trained clergy), to be catapulted into the forefront of Christian expansion.

In truth, leaders are really just "ordinary people who guide others along pioneering journeys"[10] or, as Dr. J. Robert Clinton says, a leader is "a person with a God-given capacity and a God-given responsibility to influence a specific group of God's people toward His purposes for the group."[11]

A leader is a person of strange simplicity and strange power whose life commands a strange respect and produces a strange fruit. It is the simplicity, power, respect, and fruit of the Holy. A leader can be just about anyone. Both Bishop William of Wykeham and the anonymous tree planter are leaders. In this regard, it is understood in a missional Kingdom culture that leadership is a function of each person focusing

[9] "Reformation" refers to the reforming of the Christian Church in Europe, made most popular by Martin Luther's *95 Theses*, which invited discussion on the practice of the sale of indulgences in 1517. "Radical Reformation" refers to the furthering of Luther's reformation ideas by those who became known as the Anabaptists (re-baptizers), which burst onto the European Church scene from Zurich, Switzerland in 1525. A small group led by Conrad Grebel, Felix Manz, and George Blaurock baptized themselves in opposition to the Church-State practice of infant baptism.
[10] James M. Kouzes & Barry Z. Posner, *The Leadership Challenge*, 13.
[11] Carson Pue, *Mentoring Leaders*, 96

on serving those in their sphere of influence in order for the fullness of Christ's leadership and character to take root and bear holy fruit there.

Leaders who "lord it over" others will not to have the necessary influence for the cultural and systemic Kingdom transformation exhibited in the glory of Aragorn. They will ultimately destroy what they put their hands to because it is all about them. This happens in homes, workplaces, circles of friends, and even churches. A centripetal spin tends to lead to downfall, whereas the centrifugal spin of the Christ-centered leader tends to spread blessing all around.

So for a missional Kingdom culture, leadership is not a function of title, but redeemed personhood and purpose. It is, therefore, the responsibility of all who have influence over others. We are all, with Aragorn, called to "Lay aside the Ranger" and be what we are meant to be—God's workmanship re-created in Christ Jesus (Eph.2:1-10) influencing for his glory the people and circumstances we have been brought into and planted among.

A second strange reality arising from this first corrupt leadership definition is the unrealistic expectations heaped upon those who dare venture to accept the call of the community to lead. For a missional Kingdom culture to be a reality among our churches, leaders must be seen and celebrated in their diversity. As I mentioned, my own personal experience has meant following on the heels of other leaders with very different gifts than mine. At first, being the ying to someone else's yang makes you a hero and it's all exceedingly warm and fuzzy. You are the fresh to what has become stale, which can provide the perfect diversion from your own stuffiness, mustiness, and stuck-ness. The great danger for the leader when strange truths are accepted is that it can all go to your head and you risk believing the hype. Over time, however, you are brought back to earth with a thud as the fellowship begins to ache for what it is missing and for what you, as the "fresh" leader, cannot provide to the same degree the previous leader did.

Practically speaking, this means that a congregation with a strong pastoral care presence in one season of leadership will often swing to someone with opposite gifts in the next season. The culture of the body then tends to be shaped by this never-ending pendulum, which if witnessed objectively can look eerily similar to an adolescent mood swing.

This not only confirms the first corruption we are seeking to alter, where leadership is reserved for and expected from far too few, but it also produces whole church fellowships that schizophrenically bounce back and forth for decades between opposite giftings and personalities. Meanwhile, leaders who are bounced back and forth deliver their dog and pony shows to many new towns between graduation and the grave. The consequence of this ecclesiastic swing dance is immature and directionally challenged churches, not to mention immature and burned out leaders.

Now, of course, none of the bodies I have served, leaders I have followed, nor I myself intentionally sought to perpetuate this immaturity—it's just the way we think it's supposed to be. It's not as if this swing dance has been entirely fruitless, either. Churches and their leaders have been doing great things in Jesus' name for a long time, but I would contend that the missional effectiveness and Spirit-filled dynamism of the church wanes proportionally as the professional-ization of church leadership and unbiblical expectation of her leaders increase. This is a corporate immaturity that tends to result in a lot of wheel spinning, backtracking, and stutter-stepping rather than a consistently forward Kingdom advance. One wonders how this phen-omenon has contributed to the lost cultural influence of the church in western nations.

The most helpful remedy to this dilemma is not the canning of a supposedly ineffective leader or the arrival of a Messiah-type deliverer. Though initially a new leader or programmatic panacea may provide new energy, relief, and hope, eventually the system defaults to the same problems and we're left tempted to hit the reboot button again. The only answer is a re-evaluation of our understanding of the church, her mission, and her leaders, coupled with the recovery of the priesthood of all believers.

A survey of the healthiest and most missionally engaged churches reveals that they have, for the most part, avoided this pendulum swing of which we have been talking. The ability or inability of churches to take missional faith risks for Jesus is often connected to stable and shared leadership where the culture of the faith community is shaped by a variety of long-term voices. This dynamic has produced good and lasting fruit.[12] Conversely, where the body looks to one leader alone to "do" ministry for it, or where one dominant leadership gift is relied upon, an unbalanced and immature corporate reality emerges that repeatedly produces internal conflict and limited meaningful missional engagement with the world. The corporate move in theses cases, not unlike mental illness, is a centripetal spiral into self and the loss of a healthy ability to relate to the wider context to which the church has been called.

In the end, the expectations heaped on each new leader are simply knee-jerk reactions to the previous season of ministry. This is a recipe for disappointment for both congregation *and* leader. What we have at the moment is an unbalanced and adolescent church life. Certainly what God seeks for his people is a mature engagement with a world lost in sin and self. What hope is there if the church is equally wrapped up in itself?

As we saw in the story of Bishop William and New College, there is great hope to be found in even the darkest of times when someone sees what can and must be done and puts hand to plough. Ironically, William of Wykeham's pure desire to provide an avenue where simple blokes could be equipped to fill the void of vacant church offices is once again in need of revision. I am not saying formal theological and biblical training is unnecessary (I have been blessed and formed by it myself). Nevertheless, the models we have built and grown dependant on can hamper rather than help. The models have simply become too expensive, cumbersome, and divorced from the life of the local fellowship to meet the great cry of churches in need of rapid multiplication of godly, missional leaders. When responding to the call

---

[12] For example, Tim Keller and his team have led Redeemer Presbyterian Church in New York City for 19 years, planting over a hundred churches. Oswald J. Smith shaped Toronto's People's Church into one of the most dynamic missionary churches in Canada during his 30 years as pastor from 1928-1958. Bill Hybels has served as pastor of Willow Creek Community Church in Barrington, Illinois for 33 years, producing an abundance of dynamic leaders and gifts that have been shared with the whole body of Christ. Outside North America, this pattern remains consistent: the stories of the Chinese, Korean, and Ethiopian Meserete Kristos Churches being examples.

to church leadership seems impossible for someone because of the cost and accessibility of effective education something in our methods requires reevaluation. A new complimentary partnership between local fellowship and training institution is desperately needed, and this is something that many colleges and seminaries are increasingly developing with hopeful results. We can rediscover a vision for such new development from the history of places like New College, but there is still nowhere better to turn for effective solutions than the Scriptures themselves.

In Ephesians 4, the Apostle Paul is speaking to the whole body of believers gathered in Ephesus. He calls them to live as one body beneath one Lord. The focus is the unity of the people of God and the calling the body of Christ has received to salvation and to be *the* people through which the *"manifold wisdom of God might now be made known to the rulers and authorities in the heavenly places"* (Ephesians 3:10). It is a grand and glorious vision.

In the next breath, however, Paul destroys any notion that unity and oneness is equated with sameness and the end of diversity. Eddie Gibbs points out that collaboration, the recognition that we're all in this together, is necessary but cannot be the primary value of a people. This important unity can become misguided when it is something *we* strive after. Instead, as Paul is seeking to help the Ephesians understand, unity is not something we create; it is something God creates in us as we join him in his work in the world. Gibbs says we must strive for a *synergy* in the body of Christ where we are not forced to be the same and come to the same conclusions, but recognize that our diversity is part of God's wisdom that will bring about more than we can ask or imagine.[13]

In other words, we collaborate or find consensus on the deepest values, truths, and purposes of God and his church as shaped by his revelation to us, but then freely synergize our diversity to bring about greater things. We resist the temptation to turn community into our primary value. Our primary value as the people of God cannot be what we share together, but who God is, what he has shared with us in

[13] Eddie Gibbs, *LeadershipNext*, 124.

Christ, and what we in turn are asked to share with one another and our world. Only from this Divine center is a synergy of true *comm-unitas*,[14] a community with a grand sense of purpose, possible.

So, Paul says, there is grace given to each one of us. The gifting favour of God has touched each of our lives and the ascension of Christ becomes as necessary as his coming in a manger. It is his leaving that makes it possible for more to be accomplished than even his earthly presence could. Jesus declared as much when he told his disciples that they would do greater things than he had been doing because he was going to the Father (John 14:12). Paul says Jesus left so that he could give gifts.

When Jen and I only had two children and life seemed so simple, we moved to Alberta, Canada, thousands of kilometres from our families, to serve alongside a small church family. They were wonderful people who probably blessed us more than we ever blessed them—in many ways, they nursed us back to health. Still, it may have been our two young sons who benefited most from the experience. Provinces removed from their grandparents, holidays and birthdays were met with great and lavish packages at the post office. Even worse, from the perspective of parents trying not to spoil their children, grandparent visits meant that leaving would be celebrated with some grand consumerist goodbye. The boys would receive great parting gifts because, well, that's what grandmas and grandpas love to do.

In a sense, that seems to be very near the heart of God as Paul describes it in Ephesians 4. Jesus leaves the scene, physically at least, but lavishes upon his disciples great gifts. And what are they?

> *"It was he who gave some to be apostles, some to be prophets, some to be evangelists, and some to be pastors and teachers, to prepare God's people for works of service, so that the body of*

---

[14] Michael Frost, *Exiles*, 105-29. Frost describes how the idea of *communitas* was first described by anthropologist Victor Turner in his study of the rituals of African tribes. Turner noted that in seasons and rituals of testing—among teens who were on the threshold of becoming men, for instance—that true community, which he called *communitas*, emerged. These seasons of communal liminality stretched these future leaders, caused them to rely on each other, and heightened their commitment to one another and the cause of their people as a whole.

OUR LEADERS LEAD

Christ may be built up until we all reach unity in the faith and in the knowledge of the Son of God and become mature, attaining to the whole measure of the fullness of God"

EPHESIANS 4:1-13 (NIV)

The gifts Jesus gives are people. The gifts are leaders who will equip the saints for ministry. In a missional Kingdom culture, leaders lead by preparing believers to put into action what the Holy Spirit has planted in each redeemed soul.

The separatist models of institutional Christendom removed our leaders from the local community to train them properly in order to fly them gloriously back—often somewhere else—as professional clergy who could run the institution tidily. This model assumes "real" equipping happens anywhere other than the local church. Paul, in his New Testament simplicity, implies that the equipping gifts of the risen and ascended Jesus for the church are actually present not just at some far-off institution, but right there in the local fellowship. The leadership gifts necessary for the mature life and witness of the body of Christ is not a professional service, but a people gift intended for great synergy. The focal point of equipping is the whole people of God for the sake of the grand purposes of the Church in the world, not a select few stars who can pile up degrees.

Once again, I am not advocating the abandonment of training institutions, but their reorientation. They must serve and complement local churches, not remove and confuse. Theology, once described as the "Queen of the sciences" must return to her rightful home—the Church on mission. While this can take place where there is synergy between local fellowships and training centres, the prevailing thought that equipping is best "out-sourced" is proving debilitating when the Church is increasingly floundering. Ironically, the response to this problem has been the emergence of many church leaders with entrepreneurial, business, or even trades training, but almost no biblical and theological grounding. While we should be enormously grateful for the Lord's faithfulness in raising up workers for the harvest, this too will prove unhealthy in the long-run if not synergized with the wisdom of the Church through the ages. It is striking that many truly missional movements do not lack willing, teachable, and teaching leadership, while those Church circles dependent upon the classic "out-sourcing" of leaders are struggling to find warm bodies to push through the system toward ordination.

At the heart of Paul's vision for equipping leadership is the so-called fivefold ministry of the apostle, prophet, evangelist, pastor, and teacher. Importantly, it is clear that these gift leaders to the body are not meant to do the work of ministry on behalf of the church, nor to run an institution or set of programs, but function to equip and train all of God's people for works of service. They prepare the saints for the work of ministry so that all God's children can share their uniqueness in the building up of the church. In this plan of God, the bishop and the tree planter are of equal importance.

Wolfgang Simson sees the fivefold ministry function as the "self-organizing powers of the church. They are part of the built-in 'biotic growth potential,' an internal structure, part of the spiritual DNA of the church, which forms itself within the body of Christ just as a human body forms its own lymphatic system, white anti-body system, a blood circulation system, etc."[15] It is the glorious task of those called to use their apostolic, prophetic, evangelistic, pastoral, and teaching gifts to equip a body that will be increasingly:

- Apostolic—advancing the cause of Christ through creativity and the founding of new things.
- Prophetic—faithful to what God has said and determined to remain true to God's speech, will, and plan, no matter how uncomfortable.
- Evangelistic—able to help people find Jesus and form them as his disciples.
- Pastoral—caring for the long-term and whole (spiritual, physical, emotional) well-being of the

---

[15] Wolfgang Simson, *Houses that Change the World*, 110.

sheep and nurturing healthy, Christ-centered relationships.

- Teaching—centering on and understanding the truth revealed by God in his Word, which is the life source of the body.

The role of the five-fold leaders is to model, teach, draw out, and equip these healthy and balanced dynamics that God has placed within the church like DNA. With this emphasis, maturity, mission, and unity is not only possible, but inevitable. This leadership focus draws out the true nature of the church.

One can quickly see how such a body, as Ephesians 4 declares, will be built up, attain unity, and become mature. Such a body would be able to withstand the storms and craftiness of the world that seeks to lure the growing church down wrong paths like a vulnerable teenager. Such a leadership emphasis would see a loving, fit body of Christ emerge in each locale, able to celebrate what has been accomplished together and not what a particular leader has done. And it will be the fivefold leader's great pleasure to sit back and applaud what was done through them, though not by them. In this sense, leaders in a missional Kingdom culture are midwives of Christian ministry—they simply coach, catch, and release... only to do it all over again. Our leaders, then, become spiritual parents who rejoice when the people of God say, "We have done it ourselves!"

But, what does this mean for the life of a local Christian fellowship?

First, it will mean we receive our leaders as gifts of equipping, not employees who do our bidding. The leadership gifts of Ephesians 4 are intended to train up a people. They are to identify, massage, and draw out the healthy dynamic of the body as a whole. The purpose of the leadership gifts Paul describes is to equip saints for ministry, not to do what the saints want. In truth, what the saints want—I truly believe this—is to be equipped as a missional force that will build up the body and effect Christ-transformation in their world. The Holy Spirit is aching to emerge in their redeemed person, but too few leaders and congregational systems value this equipping priority and instead default to a ministry model that is more "fee-for-service" or program director in nature. The result is frustrated leaders and a stunted body.

Second, it will mean we measure success by fruit and not performance. Leadership evaluation and reviews, whether formal or around the potluck table, tend to focus on performance criteria (i.e. "What did you think of the sermon?" or "She didn't visit so-and-so!"). This is not a biblical model. Instead, we ought to be measuring success by whether or not the fruit of a missional, orthodox, and Spirit-filled people is increasingly evident. What we are measuring then is the whole people, and not a select few. The measure of an Ephesians 4 leader, then, will be the evidence of fruitful equipping, the emergence of mature, missional unity, and not the fleeting standards of performance, titillation, or whether they've been doing what is expected. What is expected, from God's perspective, is ripe and mature fruit, not meaningless sacrifices done well.

Third, it will mean we become more communal and Trinitarian in our leadership structures. If God in his own unity is diverse, then why are we so determined to sink all our leadership eggs into one basket? The Trinity is the communion of the One True God, where diversity is not only mysterious, but seemingly necessary. To reflect God's purposes, then, will mean seeking to build leadership teams that provide the balancing voices of the apostle, prophet, evangelist, pastor, and teacher. Rather than swing like a pendulum away from one gift in search of what we're starved for, it would be better to maintain that gift while balancing the communion of leaders who equip us.

In a multi-staff church setting, this could mean staffing less by job description and more by gift description (i.e. "We've got a good pastorally-gifted leader, let's identify and call out a prophet or evangelist"). It may mean embracing a larger number of supported leaders (even if only part-time) to bring a healthy, mature balance to the equipping task necessary for a missional Kingdom culture. In churches where there is only one supported leader, or even no supported leader, viewing the elder team or overseeing the leadership body through this lens can be equally effective.

Most likely these gifts are already present in God's wisdom and grace. It may just require naming, identifying, and calling them out.

The result will be a new confidence in giving our gift (and not hiding it behind some false humility), joy in receiving another's gift, and a confession of our ongoing need for one another. I am not the whole church, and neither are you. We are the church together, a mysterious reflection of the mystery of the One God who is yet three. So leaders need the humility to accept they are not, and indeed cannot be, all things to all people and require the equipping gifts of others.

Fourth, it will mean teaching our people what it means to be leaders and opening their eyes to this fivefold reality, even in micro settings. Those who lead us must begin equipping in this direction immediately. In truth, any Spirit-led committee, team, or small group within most fellowships already operates with this divine DNA at its core, but teaching in this area can awaken new effectiveness and fruitfulness. We must invest in the equipping of each person as a leader in their sphere of influence—including homes, schools, community clubs, workplaces, and not just "church" stuff. Most likely, a body who is increasingly equipped for the ministry of evangelization, for example, will be unable to confine that mature service to a committee, event, or program. Instead, they will find that evangelization is happening where real life is taking place—most often in the seemingly small, insignificant, and micro places where Christians rub shoulders with those who have yet to name Christ Lord. In other words, the maturely equipped body will be doing effective ministry outside church building walls in greater measure.

This teaching is not rocket science, but available to all in the Scriptures. A study of what the role of each of the Ephesians 4 leadership gifts is can bring "Aha!" moments as we look around our own church fellowships. Most likely we'll discover what has already been present but has never been free to thrive or bring its influence to bear on the life of the whole body.

Fifth, it will mean becoming a learning and unlearning organism. We will need the courage to risk setting aside institutional, Christendom, and even business-world definitions of the church and leaders for more biblical ones. The Church is a unique and uncommon organism in this world and sometimes we interpret her through the wrong lenses. Our humility to confess our veiled perspectives of how leaders ought to function among us and willingness to relearn is of paramount importance to many local churches. So rather than silence the prophet or shackle the apostle, we must unlearn this tendency (which has caused apostolic gifted people to find hope in parachurch organizations and prophets to be stoned). We must invite them to bring their equipping voice to bear upon us all. We must learn to learn and unlearn. We must become an organism that can fluidly adapt to shifts in culture while remaining biblically mature. We must not remain with organizations that are stuck in old habits, too proud to put aside old wineskins.

Sixth, it will mean a new understanding of the role of the preacher. The preacher—the peculiar proclaimer of God's truth—is, if we understand Paul correctly, an equipper of a proclaiming community. The stated goal of preaching must be the development of a people equipped to carry the Good News in all its simplicity and power into those spheres of influence in which they lead. Historically, it was often the case that the proclaiming task of the gathered was a shared reality. Paul instructed the Corinthians to hear from two or three prophets when they gathered (1 Corinthians 14:29). He told Timothy to be about the task of entrusting to reliable people the message that had been entrusted to him (2 Timothy 2:2). At the heart of the preaching task and event—for it is an event when the truth of God is embodied in flesh before us and given utterance in our tongue— is not spiritual entertainment (i.e. "What a great preacher!"), but the equipping of a preaching people, a community of saints who will with their whole lives declare the glory of God wherever they are found.

Therefore, we need the teacher, pastor, and evangelist to preach in order that their unique voice shapes us like those rich in the knowledge of God and his ways, abundant in our ability to care for and nurture discipled lives and relationships, and wise in our ability to help people on the path to Jesus. These three gifts are important. But what we really need are the voices of the apostle and prophet. Paul says in Ephesians that the foundation of God's household of saints is the apostle and prophet, with Jesus as the chief cornerstone (Ephesians 2:19-20). The welcome of Jesus, it would seem, as the cornerstone upon which a Kingdom people is built, requires a foundation of apostolic and prophetic witnesses. The voice of these two gifts—one pointing us to who God is and what he demands (prophet) and the other awakening us to be about his work and Kingdom advance in the world (apostle)—provides the foundation upon which the church finds her identity and purpose for engagement with the culture it inhabits and shares the Good News with.

Interestingly, when the Church becomes centripetal and institutional, it relies almost solely on the voice of the pastor and teacher, therefore becoming unfounded and immature and actually risking being built on a foundation of sand rather than rock. With a recent history of not embracing the shared leadership task of equipping the saints, as Paul explains in Ephesians 4, the church has drifted from its overarching mandate to disciple the nations and willingly sacrificed Truth on the altar of social acceptance and political correctness. A steady diet of these unbalanced leadership gifts has resulted in mission-less and timid churches that lack the necessary impulse, backbone, and tenacity to steadily incarnate the Gospel in hostile territory. Instead, we turn in upon ourselves (which is affirmed by our over-emphasis on the pastoral voice), get lost in controversies (which the over-emphasis on the teaching gift adequately feeds), and become irrelevant to any of the saints whose call and gift does not fit this narrow focus. Evangelization then becomes either a totally foreign and frightening concept relegated to the backburner or to a program of "outreach." This abandonment of the apostle and prophet has also significantly contributed to the increasing absence of men in North American churches. Having forced the more "cutting-edge" gifts out of the local church, we have communicated to men—who are more prone to share apostolic and prophetic tendencies—that "church" is really about warm fuzzies, sharing your feelings, and learning stories on felt board. Church as an adventure, as storming the gates of hell, is hardly a vision we aspire to anymore.

A recovery of the preaching event as the moment for apostolic and prophetic utterance is desperately needed. This recovery will be the seedbed for the emergence of the other leadership gifts that are called as one to equip a proclaiming people who will be about the task of building a missional Kingdom culture. So equipped, we will be who we are meant to be, embodying and proclaiming the wisdom of God across the street and to the highest heavens, whether as titled leader or unnamed tree planter.

- Identify and describe the areas of your life where you are a leader. What strengths do you bring to that setting? Where do you need the balancing influence of another leader? What equipping could you use to be more mature in that important place of calling?

- Can you describe a time or situation when the demands and expectations placed on leaders were not only unrealistic, but unbiblical? What was the fruit thereof?

- Can you think of people in your fellowship who are apostles, prophets, evangelists, pastors, and teachers? How could your church make it possible for these leadership gifts to be more effectively engaged in equipping the whole body for maturity? What role does preaching have in this and what should missional preaching look like in these days?

For the Toolbox

In building a growing capacity to be a people who release our leaders to lead, the following tools can be effective aids in the healthy development of your missional Kingdom culture:

a. **The Ministry Cube**

We use this simple tool with our staff at Kingsfield to provide a snapshot overview of the ministry responsibilities, priorities, goals, problems, and life challenges facing those who lead the body. Having not just staff, but team leaders and elders using this can focus their ministries and help them think about the big picture, as well as holistically about their lives and missional involvement. Periodic use of this tool can create deeper personal and ministry team development since it permits space for the interaction and interconnection of the personal and corporate realities that shape groups of people.

Please use the cube diagram on the next page to give a 3D view of life for you and/or your ministry:

Out Front: What needs to be done? What tasks, relationships, priorities, or reading are before you (or our ministry/church) that demand primary attention? Are you procrastinating? What help could you use? What other people are you engaging and equipping for the task at hand? What fruit are you most excited about and praying for?

In View: What lies ahead? What tasks, relationships, priorities, ideas, and reading do you plan and hope to give time to? What vision is bubbling within you? What signs have you seen of new things God is doing? How do you need to grow to get to where you see God leading? When are you blocking time for rest, Sabbath, and prayer?

Grey Areas: What is confusing or unclear? What tasks, relationships, priorities, and questions are you wondering about? What signs or patterns do you notice that are awakening new visions or sharpening your current direction? What doubts are you currently wrestling with? What are you afraid of? Where is something seemingly impossible that God alone can redeem or transform? Who are you testing and discerning these grey areas with?

Out Back: What is hidden that shouldn't be? What do you need prayer for, want to talk about, or know others should know about (even if you don't really want them to know)? What hidden things or "elephants in the room" (things everyone knows is there but no one is talking about) need to be exposed? What personal realities are sources of joy or frustration these days? Are you feeling overwhelmed and alone? Who would you be willing to allow into this situation?

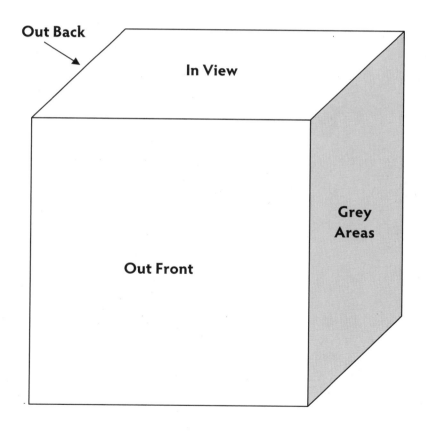

b. **Invest in Leadership Development**

Set growth expectations for leaders: Each church should plan for and invest resources in developing leaders. Setting aside dollars for pastors, elders, and other ministry leaders to be equipped through conferences, courses, and focused readings should not be an imperative.

One simple, yet excellent resource to evaluate and mature leaders is the "Leadership Practices Inventory." This tool allows for 360 degree peer feedback and builds upon the work of James Kouzes and Barry Posner's excellent study, *The Leadership Challenge.*[16]

In addition, if we expect our key leaders to grow, we should force them outside their comfort zones. The possibilities here are endless. Using your collective imaginations, contacts, and creativity will no doubt open up great ideas. One example could be the simple (or perhaps not so simple) task of having your leaders preach the gospel in a three-minute sermon. Another example of stretching that develops leadership fitness is the "Pastors to Projects" trips that Mennonite Disaster Service provides to leaders. On these trips, leaders spend a week serving in an area of North America impacted by natural disasters. Visit www.mds.mennonite.net for details.

Arrow Leadership: My own personal experience in the two-year Arrow Leadership program was invaluable (www.arrowleaderhip.org). Arrow, especially focused on younger leaders, is designed to equip leaders to lead like Jesus, be led by Jesus, and lead more to Jesus. For a church fellowship with younger leaders, encouraging and supporting this journey into mentoring and equipping will reap long-term benefits. There are other similar programs of leadership development—perhaps developed by your denomination or wider church fellowship—that

---

[16] *The Leadership Challenge* (San Francisco: Jossey-Bass, 2002). The inventory can be accessed online (www.lpionline.com).

may prove just as valuable in your context. In any event, being a people who stand by and invest in the growth of leaders who understand what it is to lead like Jesus will always be enormously fruitful. One other note: expecting leaders (especially vocational ministers) to pursue accredited education can be very worthwhile and necessary. However, there is something especially transforming when leaders are given the freedom to pursue opportunities, like Arrow, that are not necessarily burdened by the stress of graded papers and proper footnoting, but are still stretching and demanding. In short, place value on character growth, strong mentorship, biblical depth, and gift development in the forms best fitting individual leaders.

Come apart so you don't come apart: Leaders need breaks. Jesus took his disciples away for rest because he knew the demands of the crowd (Mark 6:30-31). Plan retreats regularly that force your leaders into different environments where rest and renewal are real. Most leaders (whether vocational or volunteer) are busy because of their giftedness and vision, but they are not always gifted at resting or seeing the need for renewal. Like Jesus, we may have to lead our leaders into this important discipline. Beyond the occasional retreat, also plan sabbaticals for your leaders—and not only for supported staff. Elders and committee members deserve and require seasons of rest and renewal where the load they carry can be set down or passed to someone else for a time. The long-term health of the body will be better for it. This corporate discipline will not only renew weary willing servants, but will provide for the surprising emergence of new leaders.

c. **Mutual Mentoring**
Paul D. Stanley and J. Robert Clinton state, "A network of vertical (mentors) and horizontal (peers or co-mentors) relationships is not an option for a believer who desires to

grow, minister effectively and continuously, and finish well."[17] To develop leaders who lead well, we should *expect* them to seek out and build compass relationships of mutual mentoring. Discuss who fills the following mentoring roles in the development of you and your leaders:

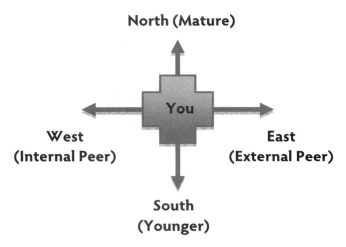

North (Mature)

**West
(Internal Peer)**

You

**East
(External Peer)**

**South
(Younger)**

Vertical *(north-south)*:
Upward—relationships with mature followers of Christ who have resources and experiences you need.
Downward—relationships with younger followers of Christ who need what your maturity and experience offers.

Horizontal *(east-west)*:
External—relationships with peers outside your church or ministry setting that help you learn new perspectives and see outside your boxes.
Internal—relationships with peers inside your church or ministry setting that build camaraderie, accountability, and foster interdependence.

---

[17] *Connecting: The Mentoring Relationships You Need To Succeed in Life* (Colorado Springs: Navpress, 1992).

Expecting our leaders to be continually sharpened by the irons of mutual mentoring relationships should not be considered optional, but an imperative for the growth of a missional Kingdom culture.

CHAPTER THREE

"I Am a Disciple of Jesus and I Contribute to His Kingdom"

Let the Kingdom Come...

Dandelion seeds thick as snow were blown along by a spring breeze as I walked my 21-month-old son to a small corner grocery store in suburban Moscow. We were in the process of completing the adoption of this, our first child, and he was learning as much about being our son as I was learning about being his daddy.

It was near the supper hour and my wife and I had learned—a mere week into this parental journey—that meal preparation always went best without our hungry son in the room. Hence the walk on this warm, sunny, windy day to get some groceries, and then on to a playground to pass time before we could safely return to a waiting feast.

Having successfully navigated grocery shopping in another language, of which I knew only enough to embarrass myself, we headed for the playground that sat in the central square of the Soviet-era apartment block that was our temporary home. Scattered throughout the play area were swings, merry-go-rounds, and small steel-frame climbers shaped like turtles that stood only a couple of feet high.

The park was full of children and adults on this beautiful evening and I tentatively entered the fray, keenly aware that my Caucasian appearance and blonde hair barely masked my non-Slavic ancestry. I was as North American as a Big Mac and everyone knew it. In fact, several of these people, and specifically one babushka, had seen us before and had kindly waved or tried their best to speak English to me on previous occasions while I exercised my limited Russian.

My son Caleb, already the daredevil he continues to be to this day, decided he wanted to go on the merry-go-round—one of those nausea-inducing child torturing devices that have always made my head spin and my stomach scream for mercy.

Another little girl of about four was already seated and spinning in circles. Her mother graciously stopped the ride long enough for Caleb to jump on, too. The dizzying motion began again, but it wasn't long before my son, the wannabe stunt driver, asked for more speed. The mother agreed and there I stood proudly as my son, my first son, spun gleefully, a huge smile on his face.

As he passed me happily for the fifth or sixth time, Caleb's toddler attention span kicked in and he decided he'd had enough. So he stood up and took one step toward disembarking. You don't need to be a physicist to visualize the result of such a move on a spinning object.

Now on the far side from where I was standing, Caleb, my cute button of a boy, became a human centrifugal projectile. Before I could budge or utter anything remotely resembling a warning in either English or Russian, he was hurled into the air with incredible ease. He landed with a mighty thud.

The bustling playground became instantly silent.

I rushed around the still spinning not-so merry-go-round to comfort my son with every eye upon me. Amazingly, he was not crying. He had a few scratches, but no major damage, and I picked him up in my arms like a good Daddy should.

By now, I was increasingly aware that we had become the centre of attention, or amusement, for an entire Moscow apartment complex. Desperate for escape, I picked up my bag of groceries to flee. Caleb was in my arms, the groceries hung off my left hand, and I began a brisk walk for cover as nonchalantly as possible. A few steps into this great escape, things went from bad to worse.

Remember those turtle climbers? My third step toward freedom came down perfectly between the bars of one of those blasted ground-hugging metal turtles. What followed ought to have been filmed in slow motion. I went down hard. The bag of groceries flew marvellously into the air like May Day fireworks. Caleb, my already shook-up and tiny son, was body-slammed into the ground with all one hundred and seventy pounds of me on top of him.

He hadn't cried before. Now he did. Actually, it wasn't really a cry; it was that scream every parent dreads because you can't make it stop.

I was utterly embarrassed. My ankle was throbbing in pain. My eggs were scrambled.

I scurried about caring for my wailing child, gathering up strewn-about groceries. Soon that babushka, whom we had seen other times in the playground under more favourable conditions, stood beside us. She spoke directly to Caleb in Russian and I knew he understood her, but I couldn't. He clung to me, yet seemed intrigued and drawn to this familiar language he heard from this grandma figure. Who could blame him after all he'd just been through with this new foreign father?

The internal tension he felt in that moment must have been excruciating. He was learning to call me Daddy, but I had just slammed him into near-oblivion. He was caught between a world he knew but was leaving and a world he didn't know if he could trust.

In the weeks that followed, this ongoing adjustment and attachment went through further fits and starts. A few days after the infamous Turtle Crisis, Jen and I watched our son roll into yet another uncontrollable crying, sweaty tantrum on the floor. His young heart and mind mourning in anguish this difficult adjustment.

This was now a daily occurrence and we were at a loss to know how to comfort and assure him. As he rolled around—dirt, dust bunnies, and dandelion seeds clinging to his sweaty brow—I slid down on the floor beside him and began to sing softly while Jen went to pray.

It seemed like an eternity, but eventually his sobbing ceased. His thumb was inserted. He rested. Then, beautifully, he crawled into my lap and rested his head on my chest, a sign of surrender. I wept and smiled. "Now we're getting somewhere, son. You can trust me. We will overcome this. And you will become the man God intended you to be."

This personal story has become a parable for me for the third of our missional Kingdom culture declarations, "I am a disciple of Jesus and I contribute to his Kingdom."

If our communities of Christ-followers are going to be truly missionally engaged in our world, we must, each of us, go through the sometimes agonizing process of attaching to the Father. This is the process known theologically as sanctification and discipleship.

As our parable reveals, this is not always an easy process, for there are times when it seems the Father is distant, ambivalent, and just plain mean. At other times, however, we know his tenderness and compassion. Growing up in our understanding that we are adopted into the family of God can be confusing, and even so painful that we might want out. At the very least, many remain very stunted in growth and development.

When this occurs, it is very difficult to state with confidence, "I am a disciple of Jesus, I belong to the Father, and I am dwelt within by the Holy Spirit." Furthermore, it becomes especially difficult to believe that we can make any contribution to this world in his name. And so, wearing this non-confidence and ambiguity as our identity, we meander through Christian life, not sure who we are or where we belong. We leave the contributions to others whom we are sure are better than we'll ever be. In all this navel-gazing, we rob ourselves, our brothers and sisters, and our Father of the joy and glory of being whom we have been re-created to be by faith in Jesus Christ.

Whereas our previous two missional Kingdom culture declarations tended to focus on corporate realities, this one, "I am a disciple of Jesus and I contribute to his Kingdom," is a necessary statement of self-identity and purpose for every believer in God's family. Each one of us needs to know we are safe in the Father's lap, known and cherished, and called to make significant contributions to his Kingdom's advance in the world.

In a missional Kingdom culture, the self is not lost; it is reborn, redeemed, and resurrected.

A KINGDOM CULTURE THAT
AFFIRMS OUR NEW IDENTITY

*It is no longer I who live, but Christ who lives in me. And the life
I now live in the flesh I live by faith in the Son of God, who loved
me and gave himself for me.*

THE APOSTLE PAUL (GALATIANS 2:20)

*Has the fellowship served to make the individual free, strong,
and mature, or has it made him weak and dependent? Has it
taken him by the hand for a while in order that he may learn to
walk by himself, or has it made him uneasy and unsure?*

DIETRICH BONHOEFFER

The Aesop Fable "The Miller, the Son, and the Donkey" is the
instructive tale of a man and his boy who set out for town with a
donkey that is to be sold at market. Along the way, they meet numerous people who freely give unsolicited advice on what they ought to be
doing with the poor beast of burden.

First a farm girl says they should ride it, so the miller sets his son
on the donkey. Shortly thereafter, a gaggle of gossiping women shout
how inappropriate it is for a son to ride while his father walks, so the
two switch places. Not much later, they meet some young travelers on
the road who mock the parental privilege they behold and so, self-
consciously, the miller lifts the son once more onto the donkey's back
and both ride together.

As the day drags on and grows hot, they come to a hilly area and
the donkey clearly begins to struggle. Seeing this, some villagers, who
must have been the local SPCA, castigate the two for this unfair treatment of animals. Once more swayed into action, the miller and his son
reverse the order and begin carrying the burro to appear more
humanely.

Crossing the bridge into town, the crowds begin to mock the
ridiculous scene. This frightens the donkey, causing it to jolt and slip
from the grasp of the weary men. The donkey falls into the river and
drowns.

Like all Aesop's fables, there is a deeper lesson to be learned from this sad story than simply how to care for your ass. Our lives are too easily and frequently shaped by wrong voices, and even lies that we accept as truth. These words of power, or even lack thereof, have disastrous consequences not only for the identity of individuals, but consequently society as a whole.

On the same camping weekend where red-sweatered Josiah was lost and found, the men and boys, tempered by the unnerving experience of the morning and worn from a long day of hiking and making sure no one else went missing, gathered around the evening campfire. I was charged with the task of imparting some meaningful nugget of truth to this weary group of males. What was I to say?

Philosopher Dallas Willard writes that "the social area of our life is meant by God to be a play of constant mutual blessing."[18] The implication is that our homes, friendships, churches, indeed any place where we interact with others is designed by our Creator as a two-way street of encouragement, happiness, and wholeness. God wills this. Our relationships are meant to be the beautiful reflection of his Triune communion. Unfortunately, this true blessing in the social spheres of life is far from the experience of many we rub shoulders with.

The reality of this sinful world and our social interaction with sinful people is that relationships of true mutual blessing are exceedingly rare. In fact, the vast majority of us have probably never heard another person speak into our lives what pleases them about us. Most of us only figure it out by trial and error.

Mostly we communicate that what pleases us about others is chiefly connected to what makes *us* happy. In other words, our joy in others is attached to our self-centeredness and need to be pleased and coddled. We're so busy chasing our own happiness that we don't even think of others as blessings unless they've done something for us. Even in the church, Christians who have experienced the unfathomable blessing of God can hardly bring themselves to look a brother or sister

---

[18] Dallas Willard, *Renovation of the Heart,* 188.

in the eye and say "God bless you." Is it any wonder, then, that we can hardly take the next step of saying, "You bless me?" Try it sometime and watch just how flushed people get and how darting their eyes become. Even more shameful is that in the most fundamental of human relationships, between a parent and a child, there is far, far too little of these spoken blessings. I know, for I am both a child and a parent.

Willard pushes us further to note the fallout of this heartbreaking reality:

> *Could the epidemic of addictions and dysfunctions from which the masses suffer possibly be related to the fact that we are constantly in the presence of people who are withdrawn from us, who don't want to acknowledge we are there and frankly would feel more at ease if we weren't—people who in many cases explicitly reject us and feel it only right to do so? Isn't the desperate need for approval that drives people so relentlessly today—causing them to go to foolish and self-destructive lengths to be "attractive" or at least to get attention—nothing but the echo of a lost world of constant mutual welcome and blessing in family, neighborhood, school, and work?[19]*

People are starved for blessing. In fact, I would venture to say that this has reached pandemic proportions in our very individualized society, infiltrating and contaminating the most important place on earth: the home. It is startling how many of us have never heard a parent say that we are a blessing to them by our mere presence on the planet—which, of course, they had a rather major role in bringing about.

The Evangelist Mark begins his Gospel curiously. His narrative of Jesus' life is shorter and more to the point than any of the other Gospel writers and it begins with a brief telling of John the Baptist's preparation of the soil for Jesus, followed by this:

---

[19] Ibid. 189.

> *In those days Jesus came from Nazareth in Galilee and was baptized by John in the Jordan. And when he came up out of the water, immediately he saw the heavens being torn open and the Spirit descending on him like a dove. And a voice came from heaven, "You are my beloved Son; with you I am well pleased."*
> MARK 1:9-11 (EMPHASIS ADDED)

This is one of my favourite passages of Scripture. In this otherwise simple moment by a muddy river, the Triune God expresses his great pleasure with himself. Maybe this sounds narcissistic and self-centered, but don't lose sight of what awaits Jesus, God the Son, at the other end of this watery starting line. He has been sent to reveal the word of life. He has come to bear the weight of sin on behalf of those who have made themselves his enemies. He is about to face temptation by a Scripture-twisting Accuser who will use God's own Word against him in an attempt to undermine this Trinitarian foray into enemy territory. He will endure betrayal and denial, and then face a most brutal cross. How wonderfully crucial, then, that God the Father would kick-off this most selfless of acts with blessing. "You are my beloved Son; with you I am well pleased." And God the Son hadn't even done anything yet, except identify himself to us.

Here's where many of us need a wake-up call, if God is our Father. Whereas the Father blesses the Son prior to any demonstration of faithful obedience, we reverse this order. This tragic reversal only reinforces what our sinful humanity is stubbornly sure of—that we must work for blessing. We live by law. We are sure every blessing must be earned. The Trinity, by contrast, lives by grace. God acts and speaks to bless prior to any sign of reciprocal love. He first loved us. It is absolutely distressing how many people have never heard a parent speak blessing over them. Inevitably, this void makes the blessing voice of a Heavenly Father fade into white noise as the speed of life accelerates and we become distracted by the myriad of other voices who beckon and clamour for our attention.

◆◆◆◆◆

So, there I stood. Grandpas, sons, and grandsons sat around a blazing inferno of a campfire on a June night in the northern wilderness. I spoke briefly about this Mark 1 shocker and then had them gather in clans, with singles adopted into a family circle where they were known. I asked one generation of men to look the next generation in the eye and speak the word of the Father to the Son, "You are my beloved Son; with you I am well pleased." They would then elaborate on this belovedness as much as possible. I sat down with my two sons and did the same.

What a blessed and holy moment this was.

I know that for some of the men sitting around that campfire, many of whom grew up in solid Christ-centered homes, it was the first time they had heard those words spoken to them directly.

A missional Kingdom culture is only possible when individual believers can join this refrain with confidence and assurance of their identity: "I am a disciple of Jesus and I contribute to his Kingdom." A missional Kingdom culture will be a community (really, a *communitas*, with a refined and united sense of grand purpose) where this new identity as a disciple of Jesus is affirmed and driven home with a gentle and strong hand.

This is, to be sure, a very personal word. It can be easy to join with enthusiasm a corporate chorus like "No one gets left behind!" or "Our leaders lead!" but asking someone to declare their identity as a disciple can be like picking the nervous child out of a classroom and asking her to explain the atom. She might know the concept, but put on the spot she draws a blank and slips into doubtful uncertainty. Flummoxed, she can hardly remember her own name.

It is my opinion that one of the most crucial needs facing the people we rub shoulders with each day is identity loss. Sin robs us of our created distinctiveness, sense of self, and perception of worth. This ever-present itch is conveniently masked in our affluent culture with toys, individual rights, bogus Facebook friendships, and instant YouTube fame. But place these searching souls in families, neighbourhoods, and cultures where emptiness abounds and finds company, we are left with one great big vacuum of purpose and meaning.

Without a sense of who we are, without assurance that our lives are not only blessed but also a blessing, we struggle to find our feet as individuals in a social world. Society is left to us barren. Even worse, we are destructively unable to offer any hopeful alternative to the tired and fearful cycle of going to bed, getting up, toiling, rearing a family, and dying. "Our society, in brief," writes theologian Stanley Hauerwas, "is built on the presumption that the good society is that in which each person gets to be his or her own tyrant."[20] Living with loss of our true identity leaves this world full of weeping and gnashing of teeth as each person pursues their own self-interest.

The confounding predicament for people in western nations is that despite our abundance, mobility, and communication tech-toys, we are increasingly isolated from one another. Even within families, or while text-messaging, we are wondering if anyone really knows us at all. Instant messaging has become the therapeutic massage of the lonely. We are a people constantly sending out an S.O.S., in hopes that someone out there might reach back and let us know we are not alone.

The United Nations forecasts a world population of nine to ten billion within a few decades. The increasing urbanization of human life will mean cities like Tokyo, Mumbai, Shanghai, Mexico City, Dhaka, and Lagos[21] will have populations themselves greater than some very wealthy nations. Even Tokyo's present day population of 35.2 million makes this one metropolis home to more people than the whole of Canada (approximately 33 million), Australia (approximately 21 million), or Switzerland (approximately 7.5 million). British economist Thomas Malthus, who must have been a hoot at a party (note the sarcasm please), predicted in 1798 that population growth would eventually outpace our ability to feed ourselves. This became known affectionately as the "Malthusian nightmare." Malthus could never have imagined today's population figures. While the reality and possibility of large numbers of people starving is a sobering thought that requires our careful consideration and just action, there is another "Malthusian nightmare" already causing the withering of many: people are starved to know and be known, and the number of the starving is rising as exponentially as the population.

---

[20] Stanely Hauerwas, *Resident Aliens*, 33

[21] According to the United Nations, Lagos, Nigeria had a population of less than 300,000 in 1950. In 2008, it has 10.9 million and it is projected that by 2015 the city will be home to 16.1 million souls.

How is this to be remedied and who will do it?

If you've ever flown at night, you will have noticed the power of just one light, even from thirty thousand feet. Then, as you approach a major city airport, the mass collection of individual lights becomes a scene of great beauty and power. This is a picture of the way in which identity, hope, and purpose can come to empty lives. It happens, as James Engel and William Dyrness say, "one light at a time."[22]

But who will do this? At the end of the day, there is only one body on the planet called specifically to the glorious task of revealing a human being's true identity—the Church, comprised of the disciples of Jesus Christ.

Jesus' farewell address prior to his ascension contains one *great* commission:

> *All authority in heaven and on earth has been given to me. Go therefore and make disciples of all nations, baptizing them in the name of the Father and of the Son and of the Holy Spirit, teaching them to observe all that I have commanded you. And behold, I am with you always, to the end of the age.*
>
> MATTHEW 28:18-20

Disciples are to make disciples. The blessed are to pass on blessing. The immersed in God are to immerse others in his identity. Our true identity must be revealed to us, for our identity is in whom we follow, revere, and espouse to.

It is shocking that Jesus leaves this monumental and eternal task in our failing and fragile hands. He formed a small band of disciples; now we continue his pattern. Disciples *go*. We are, he directs, to be in continuous onward and outward motion for the sake of people everywhere. We are to build this disciple-making upon that same act by which Jesus himself discovered he was a blessing. At his baptism, the

---

[22] James F. Engel & William A. Dyrness, *Changing The Mind of Missions: Where Have We Gone Wrong*, 82-3.

Father and the Spirit converge on the Son and speak the pleasing word. In our own baptisms, we are equally reminded of this phenomenal truth: we have become a daughter or son and are beloved and pleasing. In our making of disciples, we bring fractured, beaten-down, and identity-less souls to this place where they hear the affirmation of their true identity by the Father. This, I have witnessed, is a powerful and transforming reality for broken lives.

The task of affirming this new identity of the believer is commanded to belong to disciples already on the way. In this marvellous plan, the affirmation of the unseen Father, Son, and Holy Spirit is given flesh and blood as we enter a new family where someone, thankfully and maybe for the first time, speaks the word of blessing. A disciple who makes a disciple is the tangible evidence of the favour and blessing of God and provides an incarnational link right back to that moment at the Jordan when God spoke. The disciple, shoulder to shoulder with another soul, is proof God that still speaks. The commissioned, compassionate, and committed touch of the disciple is the touch of God on a life.

The disciple-making task is to speak into broken lives the restorative blessing word of God. When we form disciples, we are awakening the deafened ear to the Great Whisperer. This disciple-making, this blessing, this unfolding of the new identity of the Christian, is the incredible privilege of all who have named Christ Lord. This precious responsibility lies at the heart of a missional Kingdom culture. If the darkness of the world and the new "Malthusian nightmare" is to be brought to a glorious new dawn, the church must be *the* voice on the planet—in homes, neighbourhoods, workplaces, schools, and every other social setting—affirming our true identity as the children of God who bring joy to the Father.

Dietrich Bonhoeffer asks, "Has the fellowship served to make the individual free, strong, and mature, or has it made him weak and dependent? Has it taken him by the hand for a while in order that he may learn to walk by himself, or has it made him uneasy and unsure?" He is calling the community of the saints to be a people where disciple-making for the purpose of individual identity, freedom, joy, and responsibility is a core practice. Too often churches become social agencies propping people up, just another cog in the dependence machine, instead of being a discipling community where people learn who they are as blessed and how to live as a blessing.

The fellowship that does not bring the individual to that transforming moment, where their identity is found in Christ and they learn to walk as free men and women, is failing its mandate and rejecting its commission. A missional Kingdom culture will persistently, patiently, and often with long-suffering through tantrums and setbacks, walk alongside people in the footsteps of Jesus until *they* can say, "I am a disciple of Jesus! I have heard the voice from heaven say, 'You are my beloved; with you I am well pleased.'" From that seminal moment of attachment to the Father, the blessed are set free to be a blessing.

The Apostle Paul's interaction with the Galatian Christians is a beautiful study in the identity of the disciple. While we don't have time here for an exhaustive study, a panoramic sweep of the opening argument of the letter is eye-opening when we consider what it means to declare "I am a disciple of Jesus!" and form a missional Kingdom culture that affirms this new identity.

There is in the epistle a sharp contrast between what Paul the disciple knows of his own identity in Christ and the wavering life of the new churches in Roman Galatia (modern central Turkey). Paul's clarity of identity screams out from his salutation: *"Paul, an apostle—not from men nor through man, but through Jesus Christ and God the Father, who raised him from the dead"* (Galatians 1:1). Paul knows and stands by the identity given by his Caller.

Conversely, he mourns the identity loss of his friends in Asia: *"I am astonished that you are so quickly deserting him who called you in the grace of Christ and are turning to a different gospel"* (Galatians 1:6). Central to this desertion of Jesus is the voices being listened to. They had set out on a journey like the miller and his son, but had lost the plot. The Galatians have fallen prey to false teachers who are attaching law to the grace-filled call of Jesus. They have accepted a false gospel diametrically opposed to that which they first received that brought them within earshot of the blessing voice of the Father (Galatians 1:7-9). They have traded the Father's voice for human opinion and their true identities were being exchanged amidst all the bartering.

Again the contrast in identity is revealed: Paul points out that their capitulation to the law-wielding voices is because they want to save face; they want to prove they really are somebody. They are more concerned with conforming to the voice of people than being transformed by the voice of God. Paul, on the other hand, is so aware of who he is in Christ that any thought of people-pleasing is a cheap substitute for the knowledge of his belonging to the Father through faith in Christ (Galatians 1:10). He recounts his religiously zealous and persecuting past that was intercepted by grace on the road to Damascus (Acts 9). He roots that whole event in God's choice and call of grace (Galatians 1:15). Paul the disciple is no self-made man. He is adopted, chosen, and blessed by the Father for no other reason than sheer unlimited grace. And it is grace with purpose.

The former thug then recounts his adventures in finding acceptance among the disciples he had once hunted (Galatians 1:16-2:3). This journey into full fellowship, it appears, was about seventeen years in the making. What Paul knew about his own identity in the risen Jesus and the message that would make true disciples was finally affirmed by the leaders of the Jerusalem church (Galatians 2:4-10). They confirm the word of grace, the word of God's blessing in Christ that transforms lives, which Paul knew as his own experience. While the Jerusalem church affirmed the blessing Paul knew from the Father, Paul does not put special weight on their word. *"By the way,"* he says, *"their reputation as great leaders made no difference to me, for God has no favorites"* (Galatians 2:6, NLT). In other words, the identity of the disciple is rooted in the *Father's* voice alone.

It is God's very personal blessing to the individual that is affirmed by the disciple-making community. We don't give the blessing; we merely affirm that God has spoken. When the community abandons this task of speaking God's gospel of grace into lives, replacing it with law, it sacrifices its very purpose, creating a people dependent on human voices, which inevitably results in the disciple's loss of identity. The disciple-making task is to speak what God speaks and tune the human ear to the divine word. The human temptation—and this has been borne out in far too many false teachings—is to elevate our voice so loud as to drown out the Father's.

This was precisely Paul's issue with Peter. Peter apparently backtracked on grace, forgot who he was, and had to be called on it (Galatians 2:11-21). And now, to Paul's dismay, this same identity crisis had emerged in Galatia (Galatians 3:1-9). This tendency is our natural default, because grace is a gift we receive very stubbornly. Grace is foreign to us. In defiance of the disciple-destroying message of the law, which he had been rescued from, Paul virtually screams out the true identity of the believer, *"For through the law I died to the law, so that I might live to God. I have been crucified with Christ. It is no longer I who live, but Christ who lives in me. And the life I now live in the flesh I live by faith in the Son of God, who loved me and gave himself for me"* (Galatians 2:19-20). The missional Kingdom declaration "I am a disciple of Jesus!" is rooted in this glorious truth. This is the ultimate starting point *and* destination of the disciple. Paul uses the language of crucifixion to bluntly state what must take place for our new identity and life to burst forth.

To the Romans, Paul uses the imagery of baptism for entrance into our resurrected identity (i.e. immersion into the life and blessing of the Trinity by repentance and faith where we hear the Father's blessing). He writes, *"Do you not know that all of us who have been baptized into Christ Jesus were baptized into his death? We were baptized therefore with him by baptism into death, in order that, just as Christ was raised from the dead by the glory of the Father, we too might walk in newness of life"* (Romans 6:3-4). In Galatia and Rome, the starting point of the disciple's identity is the same: dying to our old identity and coming alive to who we are by faith in Christ.

The crisis in Galatia is the crisis facing the individual in society today. The true missional community will join the affirming voice of the grace-filled Father and resist vehemently the human temptation to retreat to law. When this retreat happens, we produce human religious systems, shackled clones of ourselves, and ears tuned out to the blessed Whisperer. We will not see the transformation of orphans into free daughters and sons of the King. To the Galatian church spinning its wheels, Paul shouts, *"For freedom Christ has set us free; stand firm therefore, and do not submit again to a yoke of slavery"* (Galatians 5:1). Paul the disciple invites, even commands, them back into the discipleship identity he not only proclaimed but knew personally. We must know our identity through the blessing of the Father. That we are chosen, beloved, and pleasing to him means the grace-filled lap we have climbed into is a secure place to be, rest, know, and be known.

For the individual in a fractured society of identity loss, a missional Kingdom culture will affirm the new identity as a blessed son or daughter of the Father. But how do we do this?

First, we never stray from the Good News. As we have seen, the identities of many people are marked by lies and the voices of others, even some well-intentioned, but what is desperately needed is a voice from beyond. The Gospel is the declaration from above that we become right with God and find rest for our striving, yearning souls not by works, not by the identity we earn in the sight others, but by turning from our sin to trust in Jesus Christ and his obedient and sacrificial death and resurrection (Galatians 2:16). A missional Kingdom culture is centered on Jesus Christ and his ability to save, redeem, transform, and define identity. The missional Kingdom *communitas* can't stop speaking this Good News. We invite people to die to self, however that has previously been defined, and to resurrection and newness of life. This is the simple, yet dynamite-laden message the disciples of Jesus bring to the world. This Good News is meant to be borne not only by "preachers," but by *all* disciples who are going and seeking ears to hear the blessing voice of the Father.

Second, we create more opportunities for life-on-life disciple-making. The plan of God is for disciples to make disciples. Discipleship is as much caught as it is taught. The most influential times of growth that lead to the hearing of the Father's voice happen in face to face, life-on-life interaction with others on the way. As such, a missional Kingdom culture creates opportunities for life to be lived in close proximity to one another. The family home is a picture of this corporate task of the family of God, and yet far too many churches are structured to resemble a factory or community college.

My son, my dear son whom I sandwiched into the dirt of a Moscow playground, became sentimentally known as "Pickle." I don't know why, but it stuck. As he grew, "Pickle" was used less and less until one day he came home from school and announced that he no longer wanted his term of endearment to be "Pickle," but rather "L.A. Rock."

"I beg your pardon?" said I. "Where did you get that from?"

He wasn't sure, but in search of his own identity, which is natural, he was seeking to distance himself, apparently as far away as the west coast, from his father's voice. I wouldn't let him do it. Not because I have anything against L.A. or Rock, or his search for his own personhood, but because if he bases his identity around the next fad, he will only and always be confused about who he really is. As his Dad, I have the enormous responsibility to call him back to his roots and his true identity—even if it is a wrinkled vegetable. In the end, I alone can help him know his identity, because we share life together.

A key value for a missional Kingdom community is spending time together that carries the practices of Acts 2:42-47. Discipleship ought to be apprenticeship in true life and not just a collection of religious data or the once a week gathering where we stare at the back of each other's heads. Jesus formed a crew of fishermen, tax collectors, zealots, and others who were nothing more than ordinary blokes, and turned them into world changers through face to face, life-on-life apprenticeship. Jesus and his disciples were, essentially, family. Which is why he could call Simon a "Rock" instead of "Pickle." Life-on-life disciple-making creates opportunities where we can freely and courageously speak into one another's lives and help deepen the identity that has already been spoken by the Father.

Third, we become patient students of the Holy Spirit's transforming work in God's kids. While many are drawn to the voice of the Father and his Good News, and it really is Good News, there are many whose growth into the maturity their identity promises becomes stunted. Much of this stunted Christ-life is the result of a sloppy understanding of Christian growth. In this sloppy understanding, we have climbed into the lap of the Father, relished his loving embrace, soaked in the blessing he bestows, but then failed to grow up into maturity and instead become the dependent, weak, and unsure types Bonhoeffer warned us to avoid.

Planted in the believing disciple is the Spirit of God, and this divine unction is a comforting, counselling, and disturbing presence. Jesus told us that our love for him would be seen in the fruit of our obedience to his commands (John 14:23-24; 15:9-10). The Father's blessing word to the Son resulted in his obedience, even to the cross, and our identity as a loved one must result in the same. The Father's blessing is both comfort and command. Our new confident identity is both cause for rest *and* action—we can and must be about, as Jesus described to Joseph and Mary, the Father's business (Luke 2:49).

The Holy Spirit is given as the power to bring our identity into full and mature bloom. However, just as no plant grows into fruitfulness apart from sun, rain, time, and even fertilizer, so our lives as maturing disciples will experience highs, lows, mountaintops, valleys, and even manure. As the Spirit took Jesus immediately into the wilderness to be tempted by the Devil following his baptism and blessing (Mark 1:12-13), so will we be led by this Wild Goose[23] into places of the soul we would sometimes rather not go. Because of our adoption as God's kids, however, we can rest assured that even those turns are wise moves of our pleased Father, who doesn't want to see his children suffer, but does want to see us grow up.

It is crucial, therefore, that we become wise to the patterns of the Spirit's work, so as to not only be a missional Kingdom culture that affirms our new identity and grows in it, but equally avoid discouragement. As John Newton wrote, "The manner of the Lord's work in the hearts of his people is not easily traced, though the fact is certain."[24]

To understand this certain, but sometimes not easily traced, work of the Holy Spirit in our hearts, take note of the following diagram:[25]

---

[23] "Wild Goose" was a description of the wild unpredictability of the Holy Spirit by Celtic Christians.

[24] John Newton, *Spiritual Letters on Growth and Grace*.

[25] I am indebted to Jamie Ramer, who first sketched this and did the groundwork, and the staff of Kingsfield (Tim Doherty, Dianne Loerchner, Tom Roes, and Anita Gingerich) for developing this helpful model.

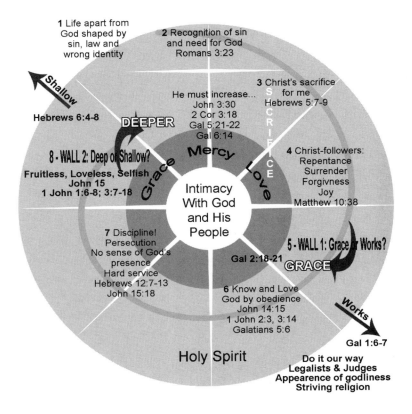

The **center circle represents** the eternal grace, mercy, and active love of God—it is the Father's lap where we rest in him and where we most intimately connect with our brothers and sisters.

Our **life apart from God** (1 on the diagram, Romans 1:18-32; 3:10-23) is corrupted by sin and shaped by law and the wrongly identifying voices of self and others. While in this state of being lost, the Holy Spirit (depicted by the lines radiating out from the center since he is constantly and everywhere active) brings two realities into full view: **The recognition of our sin** (2, Romans 3:23) and the obedient and **sacrificial life, death, and resurrection of Jesus** on our behalf (3, Romans 5:7-8; Hebrews 5:7-9).

In this divine encounter, which is the mysterious convergence of God's sovereignty, our searching, discipling relationships, and prayer by us or on our behalf, we hear the Spirit's invitation to repentance, the Son's call to discipleship, and the Father's voice of blessing. The Good News suddenly, and unexpectedly, becomes both good and true. The result of all this can be a "road to Damascus" light show as Paul experienced, or the simple, yet equally earth-shattering silent moment of surrender while standing by a lake at sunset or while stuck in traffic with horns blaring all around. However this moment of divine interception occurs, it is glorious and a tangible and palpable taste of eternity. So, **repentance, surrender and forgiveness occur** (4, John 1:12-13) and we find ourselves sitting in the Father's lap, a child of the King.

Now a Christian by the marvel of grace, we are keenly aware that we've done nothing to earn any of this blessing we've received—which is why we're on cloud nine. So, we inhale the Father's Word, the Scriptures, and come across the invitation to take up our cross and follow Jesus in order that our lives might be transformed (Matthew 10:38-39). This we are strangely and surprisingly willing and anxious to do.

Knowing our Shepherd's voice, we press on to experience his life to the fullest. However, for many, this moment becomes **a wall we are unable to get over** (5). Why? Conditioned as we are to rely on our own devices and identity to earn our way, we believe this is the point at which we begin to earn our keep. Grace and favour have been wonderful, but we know God deserves and demands more and so we determine to prove to him that he was right about us. And so, like the Galatians, we trade grace for works and risk turning away from the truth that transformed us in the first place.

If we follow the Galatians at this moment (5, Galatians 1:6-7), we move in a direction that takes us further away from true intimacy with God and one another rather than deeper into our new identity as a son or daughter of the Father. This wall becomes a place where much Christian discipleship is stunted.

If this wall is not overcome, we inevitably slip into a new legalism, which can become as binding, dark, and fruitless in good deeds than life was in a state of lostness. At least in a state of lostness darkness can be invaded by light and good deeds can reveal a soft heart moving in the right direction (remember Cornelius in Acts 10). But here, legalistic Spirit-less darkness is defended as religious light and good works are pointed to as proof that the Father must like us more than his other kids. Here the Christian becomes a merciless judge, relying on an appearance of godliness that denies its power. This is the avenue of the pitiful and pharisaic religious life which Jesus told us to avoid (Matthew 5:20).

If, however, this wall is overcome, instead of bypassed, new intimacy and fruit emerges. But how do we overcome? As always, by the Holy Spirit. First, the Spirit—whose voice drew us into the comfort of the Father's lap—commands us into **faithful obedience to the words of Christ rooted in the love of God and our neighbour** (6, John 14:15; 1 John 2:3). Faith is expressed in selfless love (Galatians 5:6; 1 John 3:14).

This time, however, our willing obedience can be met with **realities that are downright disturbing, frustrating, and disheartening** (7, Hebrews 12:7-13; John 15:18). Our service to the neighbour may prove hard and thankless. Relationships in the home and church become strained. Trials, suffering, and even persecution may bombard us. Prayer comes hard and seems unanswered. Our love for God may seem a charade. There may be no sense of his sweet presence. Even worse, we become excruciatingly aware of sins we can't shake and others we never saw before. Many in this difficult season of discipleship interpret all this as a sign that they took the wrong turn back at the wall (5). They are wrong. God is simply disciplining his kids in order to strengthen their identity. And the Holy Spirit is in the details of this period of liminality, stretching, and testing that can lead us to moments of "Argh!" and "Eureka!"

Having persevered through this stage of growth by the Spirit's power, we find ourselves at **a second wall** (8). If forgetful of our identity as the beloved and blessed, and unaware of the wise, though sometimes uncomfortable means of the Holy Spirit, we may very well miss our Father's presence and invitation back into his lap. This is another self-dying moment for the disciple. We realize our only hope—given the Spirit's unveiling of our lovelessness, sinfulness, selfishness, and fruitlessness—is to **cling to the cross of Jesus** (John 15; 1 John 1:6-8; 3:7-18). We confess all we have to offer is filthy rags. We experience with deeper awe the wonder of God's love. We know, again, that our life is truly "in" him alone. We freely boast only in the cross (Galatians 6:14) and cry with John the Baptist, *"He must increase, but I must decrease"* (John 3:30). We must take up our own cross yet again.

Many arriving at this second wall (8), however, are prone toward a different wrong turn than back at wall number one (5). There the glow of first love was still real, providing a fond memory of what could be, which unfortunately resulted in a legalistic attempt to copy what only the Spirit could produce. Suddenly facing a new wall after having been put through what can feel like a holy gauntlet, **some are tempted to completely throw in the towel.** These towel-tossers can become some of the most ardent and vocal voices against the Good News and the church. Others don't throw in the towel, but instead live in the shallows of life where a faint memory of the beauty of the Christian life nostalgically dwells. But these people become absorbed by the cares of the world. **They settle for apathy,** for token "bedtime prayer" religion and never learn to swim in the deep waters of God's grace and intimacy. These shallows lap perilously close to life apart from God (Hebrews 6:4-8; 10:15-31). This is sad and unfortunate, since a new response of wonder at the cross and honest repentance and humble surrender will mean another and even deeper affirmation of our identity as God's children, along with a deeper and more beautiful intimacy with our brothers and sisters (2 Corinthians 3:18; Galatians 5:21-22).

A missional Kingdom culture strengthens the ability to affirm our new identity as disciples of Jesus by being patient students of the Holy Spirit's maturing work in our lives. This humility can go a long way toward making sure we're all formed by his blessing voice, rather than the accusations of tyrants, becoming free to declare "I am a disciple of Jesus."

UPON FURTHER REVIEW...

- Describe ways in which your life has been shaped by the wrong voices. In contrast, when have you experienced the voice of blessing through another? When have you provided it yourself?

- Discuss the moments in your Christian growth that have been most transformational. How have you grown? In what settings? Who have been the most influential disciples in making you a disciple? How have those transformational moments reflected Acts 2:42-47?
- Take time to study the diagram on the growing disciple. Does this accurately describe your experience of the Holy Spirit's ways? Where would you place yourself on the diagram in this season of life? How can this cycle of growth also capture and describe the seasons of congregational life church fellowships experience over their history?

A KINGDOM CULTURE THAT
IDENTIFIES CONTRIBUTION

*Go from your country and your kindred and your father's
house to the land that I will show you. And I will make of you a
great nation, and I will bless you and make your name great, so
that you will be a blessing.*

THE LORD TO ABRAM (GENESIS 12:1-2)

*There is always one moment in childhood when the door opens
and lets the future in.*

GRAHAM GREEN (IN *THE POWER AND THE GLORY*)

Very few pictures of my childhood stick in my mental photo album,
but there is one I can conjure up in an instant.

My family lived on the edge of a small town. Our yard was cut in
half by a massive cedar hedge that, in my boy's imagination, was really
a castle wall. Our back door came out onto a cement patio to which
one end of this leafy castle fortress butted up against. A large cedar tree
connected to the hedge stood just off the patio, providing cover and
privacy.

One picture perfect sunny day, I ventured outside alone, which is
easy when you're an only child, and tied a skipping rope to a branch. I
was holding a wooden yardstick in my hand. This was not without
purpose. In my active imagination, the skipping rope was a micro-
phone, the yard stick a guitar, and for a few brief moments when I
thought no one was looking I was Johnny Cash, some Gospel crooner,
or whoever else it was my parents were listening to at the time. Lost in
the moment, I never noticed my mother as she stood in the doorway
and snapped a photograph of me "out front." I was leading, performing,
lending my voice. It was one of those moments when the door opens, as
Graham Greene says, and lets the future in.

I have often bantered with my parents about the winding path of
life that led me to Christian leadership. Many rides home from Sunday
worship as a child were marked with stern and disappointed conversations about my most recent desecration of that most solemn of hours.

The drive home was never long enough, because getting home meant "bottom" line consequences to which I had become very familiar—and often not without good reason. I was, I'm sure in their eyes and even my own, an unlikely candidate to oversee the flock. These days we joke that, since I could never be quiet in church, God made me the preacher.

As I grew into my teens and finally experienced the spiritual awakening my parents had been praying for, several very encouraging voices began to call me to live out with the whole of my life what that open door in childhood had hinted at years before. By age 23, my young bride and I were shepherding our first congregation. In retrospect, I know without a doubt that I would never have been ready for such a sober, joyful task had it not been for mature disciples around me. They not only helped me know my new identity in Christ, they also identified the contribution I could make toward the advance of God's Kingdom in the world.

Abram must have had an interesting father. Most Christians are aware of the amazing faith of Abram. We are all, as Paul reminds the Romans, made right with God through faith like his (Romans 4)—faith that believes what God has said and lives in response to that belief. Abram heard the voice of God calling him to leave his country and kin, and he obeyed. Genesis 12:1-2 describes the incredible commanding word of the LORD that comes to this man of Chaldean descent. It is a promise to make of him a great nation through which all peoples on earth would be blessed. What is easily overlooked is that there was something in Abram's early years that opened the door for a faith-filled future. That something was a move by his father, Terah.

> *Terah took Abram his son and Lot the son of Haran, his grandson, and Sarai his daughter-in-law, his son Abram's wife, and they went forth together from Ur of the Chaldeans to go into the land of Canaan, but when they came to Haran, they settled there.*
>
> GENESIS 11:31

Whatever it was that caused Terah to head west to Canaan, only to stop short and settle for Haran, we do not know. We are not told what circumstances led to this sojourn. We are not told what conversations around the nomadic campfire cracked open Abram's heart to a land he had never seen. What we do know is that when the LORD whispered his invitation to Abram to "go," the son of Terah was ready. He knew the voice. The pump was primed, the step out in faith somehow prepared because the community he grew up in was already, even if only subconsciously, on the move. Without taking anything away from the faith with which Abram responded to God's call, there is no denying that the voice of the LORD in Abram's life was somehow related very closely to the lifestyle of the people he knew. His own unique call and identity was providentially set in motion before he knew the Father's blessing. The blessing he was to be was mysteriously linked to the blessing of the clan-community he had received. God does nothing in a vacuum.

As we saw in the previous chapter, a missional Kingdom culture affirms our new glorious identities as daughters and sons of the Father. The whole community equips us to say that very personal word, "I am a disciple of Jesus!" In this chapter, we take the next step to understand how a missional Kingdom culture exists to identify the contribution each disciple is called to offer the forward advance of God's people.

The word to Abram is that God will bless him. Again, like the Father's word to Jesus at his baptism, this comes out of the blue. As far as we can tell, Abram has done nothing to earn this promise and blessing. It just comes and he has ears to hear and a will to obey. Abram's identity is in God's word to him. He will become a great nation and bless all peoples. This will apparently be despite the fact that at the moment of the divine declaration Abram and Sarai have a grand total of zero children. It will be this trust against all odds in what God says that is declared to be saving faith; *"And he believed the LORD, and he counted it to him as righteousness"* (Genesis 15:6).

The whole of Scripture then underlines the eternal import of this "saving faith." To believe God, to believe he loves this messy world and sent his Son (John 3:16), to trust that Jesus is the resurrection and the life for all dying souls and bodies (John 11:25-26), is to know God and be right with him. If this saving blessing to Abram's faith applies to us, then certainly the companion word of the LORD to him does as well: "You will be a blessing." Our identity as one who belongs to and pleases the Father is brought to fulfillment in the blessing we are to be to the communion of saints and the world. We have a contribution to make. "I am a disciple of Jesus and I contribute to his Kingdom."

A missional Kingdom culture that asks leaders to equip the saints for ministry cannot accept anything other than each disciple contributing to the blessing God's people are called to be to the nations. If the church is Noah's ark in a drowning world, an allegory the church fathers enjoyed using, then it is "all hands on deck!" Unemployment, passive spectatorship, is unacceptable in a missional Kingdom culture. In fact, a missional Kingdom culture cannot admit that non-participatory discipleship is discipleship at all.

The eighteenth century Moravian church leader Nicholas Von Zinzendorf declared, "I concede no Christianity without brotherhood." By brotherhood, he did not mean warm feelings of some fireside oneness, but the offering of ourselves as a blessing with our gifts, time, and resources. It is simply not possible for genuine faith to remain merely a personal, private matter. The blessing word of the Father is not just for me and my private devotional life.

If we have received the Father's blessing, if we are his kids by faith like Abram's, then we are saved, filled with the Holy Spirit, taken through the various seasons of Christian growth, and even dropped in our clans and contexts to be a very specific and visible blessing. The Good News is that we don't have to work for the Father's blessing. The Good News, section two, is that we are now commanded to be his blessing for the sake of the world. In Galatians, Paul is as equally thrilled about his unworthy identity as a son of the Father as he is about the task given to him *by* the Father. The two blessings are as indivisible as two sides of a coin.

The promise to Abram that his identity means blessing is a pledge to us as well. This is both an individual and corporate reality.

One of the heart-wrenching agonies for leaders in any church community in these post-Christendom days is the disturbing awareness that we are propping up a religious system that encourages non-participation. A misunderstanding of leadership, as we saw earlier, has erected a professional elite asked to "do" ministry for the people. Sadly, too many of us who have taken on this impossible irresponsibility have been unwilling to reject the notion. We have even perpetuated this unbiblical clergy/laity divide to stroke our own egos. A half century ago, Karl Barth lamented, "The term 'laity' is one of the worst in the vocabulary of religion and ought to be banned from the Christian conversation."

What is remarkable is that even Anabaptist and other free church[26] traditions that were founded on the prophetic dismantling of this divide and the wondrous blessing of the "priesthood of all believers" have been sucked into the whirlpool of this language and understanding.

The historian Donald F. Durnbaugh, in studying the reformation of the sixteenth century, notes that the radical reformers[27] did not abolish the ministry; they actually recovered it. He writes, "It would be fairer to say that they abolished the laity. All ... were to be ministers. Baptism for them was ordination for ministry, as well as a sign and witness of their conversion."[28] And yet today, in my own Anabaptist denomination, one of several ministry tasks both congregations and pastors are asked to rank in order of importance is "developing the ministry of the laity." That this even warrants consideration is questionable ecclesiology and a denial of our own spiritual heritage. It should simply be an expectation that what our apostles, prophets, evangelists, pastors, and teachers are *primarily* called to do is equip all the saints for ministry (remember Ephesians 4).

A further contributing factor to our emerging tradition of non-participation is our warped understanding of worship. Our emphasis on worship *services*—as something led for us that we consume—has

---

[26] "Free Church" refers to those church movements that were not aligned with the State.
[27] "Radical Reformers" is the title given to the leaders of the Anabaptist element of the sixteenth century reformation, such as Menno Simons.
[28] Donald F. Durnbaugh, *The Believer's Church,* 266.

eroded the biblical notion of worship *as* service. Our tendency to view everything as consumers, including spirituality, means we expect "church" to be a place where we receive something. My offerings are a fee for service. Worship is something I go to.

Our institutional Christendom models have, unintentionally I want to believe, undermined the truth that the church is a worshipping people joined together in the glorious task of giving something away. We are a people whose worship is not an event attended, but a blessed life lived as blessing. We have been called out of our own lands and clans to trust God with our futures. He has shaped our new identity and we are to be a blessing to the world. Unfortunately, many of our present forms do not emphasize this, but perpetuate and model that worship is wall-locked and bound to our professionals, performances, and liturgies. Worship as service, rather than merely *services*, does not mitigate the importance of the church gathering to praise God and encourage one another. Rather, it restores worship to its rightful place—the whole life of a whole people—and reawakens our joy when we are gathered to refuel in praise, adoration, and exhortation.

Through the prophet Isaiah, the LORD reprimands his people for meaningless worship rituals that are not matched by a life of service to each other and the world. The very offerings and communal rituals God instituted among the people to train them in his ways he now despises, *"Your new moons and your appointed feasts my soul hates; they have become a burden to me; I am weary of bearing them"* (Isaiah 1:14).

At the heart of God's promise to Abraham is that God is most blessed when we are a blessing to the world. God's great requirement from his people, spoken through the prophet Micah, are neither polished services nor sanitized consumerist gatherings, *"but to do justice, and to love kindness, and to walk humbly with your God"* (Michah 6:8). When Paul reflects with celebration on the great mercy of God shown toward sinners in Jesus Christ and the new identity that is ours he declares, *"I appeal to you therefore ... by the mercies of God, to present you bodies as a living sacrifice, holy and acceptable to God, which is your spiritual worship"* (Romans 12:1). For the Lord who is worthy of our praise, worship is clearly something far more substantial than we have allowed it to be.

When worship services replace worship as service, the inevitably result is the emergence of a priestly class that does for us what the rest of us can't. So, without intending to, we slip into a pattern that, by the slyness of our Enemy, subtly erodes the blessing to the nations that the whole of God's people is intended to be. Instead of being a people whose collective worship lives cause people to praise our Father (Matthew 5:16), we confine "worship" to a room where the world can't see it. In the end, you wonder how many will say, along with the "patient" of the demon Screwtape in C.S. Lewis' *Screwtape Letters*, "I now see that I spent most of my life in doing neither what I ought nor what I liked."

So deep is this worship confusion in churches today that such talk as this becomes very threatening to our very identity as believers and fellowships. We have been learning, however, that our identity is in the Father's blessed word to us, not in our acts toward him. We are therefore free to allow our discipline of gathering for worship, which is still necessary for a missional Kingdom culture to flourish, to be more real and authentic.

I am not proposing we abandon our meeting together; I am asking that we redefine them with biblical purposes in mind. When the writer to the Hebrews encourages Jewish Christians not to give up meeting together, he uses Old Testament worship imagery. We are to enter the Most Holy Place, but this is the spiritual reality of each believer who is at all times ushered into the very presence of God through the blood of Christ. The meeting of the blessed is then for the purpose of spurring one another to be a blessing. "Let us consider how to stir up one another to love and good works, not neglecting to meet together, as is the habit of some, but encouraging one another, and all the more as you see the Day drawing near" (Hebrews 10:24-25).

The meetings of missional Kingdom communities will therefore be truly *for* worship, *for* the purpose of praising our creating and redeeming God, while encouraging, inspiring, and spurring each other on to be the mature blessing in the world the Father intends his children to be. Worship that does not do this is actually not worship at all but merely the empty and meaningless sacrifices God hates. Furthermore, this rebooting of our confusion of worship will go a long way to muting many of the controversies that bubble to the fore when "services" turn merely into "preferences."

The discipline of Christian worship must truly be recovered as a discipline. The sporadic infrequency of Christians gathering in recent times is a sign that we increasingly understand worship as something consumed. Our patterns betray that at the core of our lives is consumership, not discipleship. The great reason we gather is to intentionally discipline ourselves to unlearn our old identity and be encouraged for the upstream vocation of blessing that is the life of the believer. So an ongoing conversation must emerge about what worship that is focused on being a blessing, rather than receiving a blessing, looks like. How will our gatherings form a worshipping people and not reinforce a biblically bankrupt worship/service and clergy/laity divide?

The fallout of all this theological and ecclesial brain cramping is a new identity crisis. Having told disciples that all are equal in the Father's lap, that all can hear his blessed whisper, we proceed to portray to them in practice that some are really more special and more useful to the Father than others, a notion Paul himself threw out the window in his letter to the Galatians (2:6). A genuine missional Kingdom culture will, therefore, not only affirm our new identity as disciples, but be a *communitas* where each disciple's contribution is identified and set free.

It has been said that a hockey game is twelve people feverishly exercising in need of a rest, while thousands watch restfully who desperately need exercise. This non-participatory participation may be the reality for couch potato goalies, armchair quarterbacks, and wannabe superstars, but it cannot be the reality of the people of God. A missional Kingdom culture pulls people from the bench and the stands and engages them in ministry because their new identity is intended to bless the world.

How do we do this? How does a missional Kingdom culture identify and spur on worship-filled contribution?

First, we recognize that we are truly a body. Paul goes to great lengths to correct the Corinthian confusion about gifts and whose gifts matter most. *"Now there are varieties of gifts,"* he says, *"but the same Spirit; and* *there are varieties of service, but the same Lord; and there are varieties of activities, but it is the same God who empowers them all in everyone. To each is given the manifestation of the Spirit for the common good"* (1 Corinthians 12:4-7). The diversity of God's children is intended to be a gift for the good of all. Yes, some gifts will appear to have and even be treated with greater prominence (e.g. 1 Timothy 5:17, in which Paul instructs the church to make it financially possible for teachers and preachers to do their necessary work for the sake of a people on a mission). Other gifts will be far less visible, but no less important. The emphasis is on the maturity of the body, which is seen in the church's ability to bear fruit and walk in maturity under one head, Christ. The first step, then, for identifying contribution is recognizing that no part of the body is unnecessary *and* that no part can remain inactive and isolated from the rest. This is going to demand a new humility by some of us and a new commitment to step up by others.

Furthermore, in recognizing that we are truly a body, we welcome and embrace the contributions of all ages. We tend to segregate the ages, despise the passionate immaturity of youth (which Paul counselled Timothy not to take personally, 1 Timothy 4:12), and place false parameters on those who get to contribute. Youths need mature adults in their lives, but adults need young people, too. Mentoring and discipling can and should go both ways. Historically, some of the greatest movements of the Spirit in the Church have been initiated and led by very young people.

In addition, those on the margins of society (the poor, the immigrant, or those with physical, emotional, and developmental disabilities) often get shafted and smilingly ignored in our race to get things done in Jesus' name. To recognize the body of Christ means that we receive from all people that God has seen fit to bring into his Kingdom clan. The disabled and marginalized have much to teach about faith and grace. With the incredible growth of the Church in the developing world, North American Christians may be blessed to find themselves on the receiving end of a new mission of renewal from the very places they once only thought as pagan. To recognize that we are truly a body means setting aside our ungodly prejudices and racism to be recipients of Kingdom contributions from all God's children.

Second, we actually get to know one another as brothers and sisters. Many churches recycle people through committee structures. Very often, "new" people can hardly break into our closed circles. Usually this is not out of callousness, but the result of lack of relationship. Furthermore, teams or committees that work to slot people into jobs can hardly find enough warm and willing bodies. Once more, the issue is that we actually don't know each other. Furthermore, we can be more concerned with getting tasks done than with knowing and releasing people. The gifts necessary to edify the body and bless the world are placed by the Spirit among us; we just don't see them, because we don't see each other. Spending more time in life-on-life disciple-making would go a long way in knowing one another as family with gifts to be shared. Having the courage to discuss whether we're behaving like a family or a corporation might be energy well spent.

Furthermore, getting to truly know one another can lead to breakthroughs where one disciple, by the wisdom of the Spirit, is able to identify a moment in a brother or sister's life where the door opened and let the future in. Often we are blind to these beautiful forecasts until someone who knows us points them out on the radar of our life. Being awake to the themes, patterns, and passions of a disciple's life can help us identify previously unknown areas of Kingdom contribution.

Third, we redefine what we mean by contribution. Because of our Christendom institutional churchianity, most of the people gifts of the church have been relegated to roles focused on committees or teams that run programs primarily focused on Sunday mornings, or whenever the primary meetings of the people take place. An interesting congregational study would be to figure out how many people hours go into running this very small portion of the body's life and function. We might discover that we are very unbalanced in the distribution of gifts, in light of the blessing we are called to be. A disciple is making a contribution to the advance of God's Kingdom with their uniqueness at *all* times and in *all* places. To relegate that to an institutional church structure, even a well designed one, is to put unbiblical constraints on Jesus' very diverse and scattered body.

What is striking about the New Testament description of gifts is that most of them do not fit well on a committee (Romans 12:3-8; 1

Corinthians 12:27-31). They are actually best accepted and released, not controlled and planned. One wonders how our structures hinder the creativity of the Spirit instead of channelling it. Can our structures become fearful attempts to control the Spirit's wildness? I'm not proposing mass chaos—that would need to be brought into check. What I do propose is that we accept that the work of the Spirit is best done in spiritual ways. When we disciple people to know their true identity, they will live out of that identity with humility, love, and grace and for the good of the body, not themselves. Some of the greatest contributions might actually be taking place outside of our structures. Even further, some may be happening in unlikely places where lives are really being touched—like the marketplace, the school, the backyard, the factory, the community club, and the arena or sports field. A missional Kingdom culture identifies the contribution that each member has to give to the advance of God's blessing to the world and then seeks to nurture and encourage that contribution for God's glory.

Fourth, we continue to ask our leaders to be equippers. We spent time unpacking this previously, but it should be reiterated here that if we are not asking our leaders to be equippers of the saints, we will fail to identify and release contributions. This can only hinder our mature and Christ-centered witness to the world. A focus on the equipping task of our leaders will provide a spiritual guard against the fear we might have that the gifts might run wild if we freely identify and release. Paul's correction of the Corinthian chaos, after all, is centered on theological foundation building, not structural and organizational solutions.

Fifth, we consider our context and the corporate blessing we uniquely bring to the times and places God calls us. If it is our Father's great desire to whisper his blessing to more and more people, we must also know that he will, by his Spirit, put his body together in ways intended to accomplish that task. Knowing this will free us from being bound by the ways of the past that may have adequately served their purpose at one time, but no longer do. These once worthwhile ways may now be hindering contributions rather than identifying and releasing them. The essence and spiritual nature of the gifts given to disciples has not changed since the days of the early church, but the context sure has. Hence, identifying the blessing contributions of one another and releasing them for our day will require biblical depth, cultural awareness, and the courage to say with Paul,

> For though I am free from all, I have made myself a servant to all, that I might win more of them. To the Jews I became as a Jew, in order to win Jews. To those under the law I became as one under the law (though not being myself under the law) that I might win those under the law. To those outside the law I became as one outside the law (not being outside the law of God but under the law of Christ) that I might win those outside the law. To the weak I became weak, that I might win the weak. I have become all things to all people, that by all means I might save some. I do it all for the sake of the gospel, that I may share with them in its blessings.
>
> 1 CORINTHIANS 9:19-23

A missional Kingdom culture affirms the blessed identity of the disciple. That culture then identifies and releases the contribution each disciple is created and gifted by the Holy Spirit to make. In this way, the blessing of the Father flows to the nations through the unique contributions of the whole of God's people, just as God promised to Abram.

UPON FURTHER REVIEW...

- Can you think of a time in your life when the door opened and let the future in? How has that moment been identified and nurtured into blessing? How can you do the same for others?
- What is the difference between worship as service and worship services? What practices might shape a missional Kingdom culture's worship together that will disciple a blessed and blessing people?
- How might your church fellowship create avenues by which people are better known in

order to identify and release their unique Kingdom contribution? Are your structures and expectations limiting or freeing these gifts?

In building a growing capacity to be a people aware of their identity as disciples of Jesus who contribute to his Kingdom, the following tools can be effective aids in the healthy development of your missional Kingdom culture:

a. **Know Thyself**

    Many excellent resources help people identify personality types, natural passions, spiritual gifts, and what their identity is in Christ. Few, however, are as comprehensive and well-rounded as *LifeKeys: Discover Who You Are.*[29] This tool combines biblical depth, mentoring relationships, and self-awareness and assessment of natural gifts, spiritual gifts, personality type, passions, values, and choices to develop and draw out a disciple's uniqueness. Working through this book, especially in a group setting and at a deliberate pace, awakens self-understanding and equips the body to appreciate and call out the gifts and strengths of one another.

b. **Steep in the Scriptures**

    There is nothing better to affirm the new identity of Christ in a disciple than a consistent steeping in God's word. Just as our identity is formed as our parent's speak to us, so our Heavenly Father's speech makes all the difference. Knowing his voice in Scripture tunes our ear to his voice at all times. The following Scripture studies are wonderful ways to deepen the life of the disciple in the Scriptures:

    *   Wonderfully made (Psalm 139:13-14).
    *   Of great worth (1 Corinthians 7:23).
    *   Eternally alive (John 6:40).

---

[29] Jane A.G. Kise, David Stark, and Sandra Krebs Hirsh, *LifeKeys: Discover Who you Are* (Minneapolis: Bethany, 1996). For more information, visit www.lifekeys.com.

- Created to do good works (Ephesians 2:10).
- Loved (John 3:16).
- Chosen (Colossians 3:12).
- Rescued (Matthew 20:28; Galatians 5:1).
- Child of God (John 1:12).
- Trained as a daughter/son (Hebrews 12:7).
- Forgiven (Colossians 1:13-14).
- Given God's peace (John 14:27).
- A new creation (2 Corinthians 5:17).
- Free from condemnation (Romans 8:1).
- A saint (Ephesians 1:1).
- Righteous and holy (Ephesians 4:22-24).
- Able to approach God (Ephesians 3:12).
- Complete in Christ (Colossians 2:9-10).
- A temple where God lives (1 Corinthians 6:19-20).
- An heir with Christ (Romans 8:17).
- A member of Christ's body (1 Corinthians 12:27).
- A citizen of heaven (Philippians 3:20).
- An alien and stranger in this world (1 Peter 2:11).
- An enemy of the devil (1 Peter 5:8-9).
- A minister of reconciliation (2 Corinthians 5:18-20).
- Given hope and a future (Jeremiah 29:11).
- Salt and light (Matthew 5:13-16).
- No longer living for self (Mark 8:34, Galatians 2:20).
- Living by Christ's strength (Philippians 4:13).
- Called by name (Isaiah 43:1).
- He will come to take me with him (John 14:1-3).

A Life That Grows: At Kingsfield, we have developed two daily Scripture reading guides called "A Life That Grows." They ground the believer in the story of Scripture— Genesis to Revelation—over four months. There are beginner/children (about one chapter per day) and advanced/adult (about five chapters per day) versions. The guides are available by accessing the Kingsfield website, where you can download them under "Resources."[30] There are, of course, other such tools available and you can develop your own as well. The key point is this: a disciple's life grows exponentially when immersed in God's Word.

c. Appreciative Inquiry

As a corporate exercise, appreciative inquiry enables a congregation to take special note of the positives it has to share with the world and reframe the negatives that can sometimes dominate our vision. This tool is a very helpful way of recognizing the unique contributions the mix of disciples God has put together in your context can make together.

Appreciate inquiry zeroes in on four "D's": *Discovery* (asking what gives us life), *Dream* (imagining the future together), *Design* (developing steps for healthy transition), and *Destiny* (active learning and putting what we've learned into practice).[31]

One caution: while very helpful for organizational revitalization, this tool requires the church to accomplish theological work as well. Appreciative inquiry is primarily a business model that must be influenced by the biblical paradigms of the body of Christ to be truly transformational for growing a missional Kingdom culture.

---

[30] For resources, visit www.kingsfieldcommon.ca/resources/articles.
[31] For more, check out the work of David Cooperrider and his associates at www.appreciativeinquiry.case.edu.

CHAPTER FOUR
"We Exist for the World Our Lord Came to Save"

Let the Kingdom Come...

Nestled along the winding Thames River in Southern Ontario is the very sleepy and small Moravian Indian Reserve, also known as Moraviantown.

I picked my way through the back lanes of this area one bright spring day to learn more of its quiet secret. Tree-lined narrow roads, cornfields, and simple homes dot the reservation. It is really no "town" at all. One main intersection is easily missed at the center of the community. Further down the road, an old seemingly ignored clapboard chapel, its white paint peeling and identified only by a historic plaque, overlooks the meandering Thames on its steady course towards Lake St. Claire.

The plaque tells the story of how this plot of land—today home to only four hundred people—became a haven for the beaten and weary Turtle Clan of the Delaware First Nations people and their European Christian brothers and sisters.

In 1732, Christian missionaries from Count Nicholas von Zinzendorf's colony in Herrnhut, Germany burst upon an unsuspecting world.

Zinzendorf's vision was for the Church to be a people of every tribe and nation who lived differently in the world in obedience to Christ. They were a holy nation, not bound by political or national borders. This conviction caused the Count to open his large estate in 1722 to persecuted peoples from Moravia and Bohemia (present day Czech Republic). They became known as the Moravian Brethren. The Moravians were an ethnically and religiously eclectic group—Lutherans, Calvinists, Roman Catholics, Free Church, and Hussite believers created a smorgasbord of saints and a recipe for conflict. A significant spiritual revival in 1727, based in prayer and obedience to Scripture, bridged these divides and resulted in an almost unprecedented agenda to help others and take the love of Christ to the nations. Zinzendorf, originally set apart to be a lawyer by his parents, became this amazing community's spiritual leader, as well as their political protector.

While in Denmark in 1731, Nicholas encountered Inuit believers and his heart was stirred for the world in a new way. Not long thereafter, an escaped African slave from the West Indies was brought to Herrnhut, where he told of the horrendous and inhumane treatment of slaves. This disturbed the Moravians immensely and two ordinary men, John Leonard Dober, a potter, and David Nitschmann, a carpenter, became the first of the Moravian Brethren to lay down their lives for the Lamb.

A desire to reach the world for Christ was not absent in Christian Europe in those days, but it was very closely linked to the expansion of Empires. Hence, imperial missions were wrought with blurred lines, mixed motives, and practices with lingering and fateful consequences. The Moravians were different. Flavoured by their own history of suffering at the hands of numerous "Christian" states, spurred on by Zinzendorf's vision and passion, and salted by their spiritual and communal life together, these people—numbering no more than a few thousand—literally circled the globe.

On October 8, 1732, Dober and Nitschmann boarded a Dutch ship for the West Indies. Their cry of encouragement as they left port became the theme of a worldwide Moravian life, "May the Lamb that was slain receive the reward of His suffering." The astonishing goal of these two men was to sell themselves into slavery in the Caribbean so African slaves could see and know the love of Jesus. They would suffer at the hands of their own people for the sake of the oppressed. Within 18 months, Dober was dead. Nitschmann pressed on near the breaking point. Finally, in 1733, eighteen more Moravians joined him on the island of St. Thomas. By 1737, the first Moravian congregation, called New Herrnhut, was planted and the vision of Zinzendorf and the example of a potter and carpenter took root. The Moravians became the first Christian denomination prior to the abolition of slavery to baptize slaves, a move which set them at great odds with the predominant European mindset that had strayed so far from the New Testament vision.

Soon Moravians were scattered throughout the West Indies and could be found sacrificially serving peoples in Greenland, Africa, South America, India, the United States, and Canada.

In North America, they particularly befriended and lived among aboriginal peoples. They gained respect for their non-violent, compassionate, incarnational way of life. They did not treat the native populations as other "pale faces" did and regularly suffered with the peoples they loved. The Turtle Clan of the Delaware was one such nation.

In 1782, a massacre of ninety Christian Delaware Indians, including 34 children, by white settlers in Ohio forced a difficult migration northward. The European Moravians, led by David Zeisberger, who had lived among the Delaware for nearly forty years, were powerless to stop the carnage. Despised by their own compatriots, the Moravians joined the exodus in search of a safe home.

The mixed band moved to Michigan and eventually settled in 1792 on that flat parcel of land along the Thames in southwestern Ontario. The Moravians developed the first dictionary of the Delaware language and wrote sermons and hymns in the Munsee Delaware tongue, which continues to be preserved, though just barely. The language and identity is quickly disappearing. Eventually, the Europeans at Moraviantown died off or moved elsewhere. Nevertheless, the Delaware peoples of Moravian Indian Reserve still follow Jesus and keep the stories alive of white missionaries who travelled with them to Canada and safe refuge on the green, bushy banks of a river that was once home to neither Delaware nor Moravian.[32]

That white chapel has seen better days. I don't even know if worshippers still gather there. The small reserve is facing its share of challenges in a twenty-first century world so far removed from, but not always that different from, the eighteenth century.

As I stood there, alone in the spring sun, I wanted to weep for what was, what was lost, and what yet could be. A weathered blue and gold historical plaque stands as a window into a beautiful past that surely can still be the present when Delaware Indians, European Moravians, and you and I follow Jesus together.

---

[32] The piecing together of this story is the result of numerous sources, but the most helpful were www.moravian.org, www.moravianyouth.org, "The Vanishing Voice of the Lenape" (Steve Chambers, November 17, 2002), www.nj.com, "Keepers of a Lost Culture" (Steve Wick, April 14, 2008), www.newsday.com, and www.watchword.org.

◆◆◆◆

This centuries-long story becomes a living parable of a missional Kingdom culture that declares, "We exist for the world our Lord came to save." A forgotten history opens the door to a deeper understanding and embodiment of the life of Jesus as a people appointed to join God's mission in the world.

What can we learn from Moraviantown?

First, to join God in his work is a life task, not simply a program or charity we participate in. The Moravians model for us lives available to the in-breaking of the Kingdom of God on earth. One legend has it that the Moravians took two things with them on their journeys to the uttermost parts of the earth—a Bible and a headstone. They were shaped by God's Word and prepared to die for it. Transformed by the grace of God, the cross, and the power of the Holy Spirit experienced in *communitas* with others, a life of sacrificial obedience provides tangible evidence of the Kingdom of God. It is *God's* Kingdom we are privileged to embody with our lives and even our deaths. Jesus' identity with us becomes the method by which we too engage the world. We incarnate ourselves like Dober and Nitschmann. We throw ourselves into unflinching support, as the many who stayed behind at Herrnhut did. Our lives are the medium of God's message and mission.

Second, joining God in his work will inevitably pit us against the political and religious powers that be. The Moravians often stood agonizingly alone because neither the interests of the State nor institutional Church could tolerate their Kingdom culture. This has consistently been the mark of historical movements that truly grasp the heart of God for the world—they have a truly foreign agenda in this world that is remarkably transforming. Genuine missional movements have a vision that is earthly and heavenly, already and not yet, micro and macro, and this is terribly disconcerting to the self-proclaimed systems and dominions of the planet. A people who exist for the world our Lord came to save embrace a battle that is not against, but for, flesh and blood (Ephesians 6:12).

Third, to join God in his work produces an uncommon unity. Herrnhut was a mosaic of diversity, yet a portrait of the breathless expanse of God's vision for the world. The latent racism, prejudices, and snobbery that so easily cling to all people can unknowingly linger in our hearts. This cancer is only eradicated as God's vision becomes realized in the selfless action of those working together in order that the Lamb may receive the reward of his suffering for all.

Fourth, Moraviantown in my neck of the woods stands as an example that what we do in the heat of our own times in the name of Jesus has lasting and lingering impacts on generations yet to come. Where will be the plaques dedicated to the selfless engagement in God's mission in our own day? Who will visit the places we leave behind to wonder and marvel and tell our stories? Whose future will be different because we existed for the world our Lord came to save?

A KINGDOM CULTURE THAT
UNDERSTANDS THE TIMES

*Of Issachar, men who had understanding of the times, to know
what Israel ought to do...*

1 CHRONICLES 12:32

*Something's happened... there's been a change... some shift in
values.*

ELIZABETH II (IN *THE QUEEN*)

There seem to be times when the Living God, who by his own test-
imony does not change (Malachi 3:6), nonetheless appears to
unapologetically chart a new course. For we finite bipeds, this is
exceedingly confusing and disconcerting. Or is it meant to bring holy
adventure to our tedious predictability?

We want a safe, tamed, and controllable deity. This is why idolatry is always such a tempting option. At least the gods of our own
creation can be kept to our liking and do our bidding. But God is no
tame lion. In his wonderful children's story *The Lion, the Witch and the
Wardrobe*, C.S. Lewis captures the wild unpredictability of God delight-
fully. Peter, Edmund, Susan, and Lucy are introduced, after a scrump-
tious dinner with Mr. and Mrs. Beaver, to the existence of Aslan, the
Great Lion. They have never met this big cat the Beavers so revere.
They know nothing of him and don't know what to expect. The
perplexing conversation prompts Susan to ask,

> "Is he—quite safe? I shall feel rather nervous about meeting a
> lion."
>
> "That you will dearie, and no mistake," said Mrs. Beaver;
> "if there's anyone who can appear before Aslan without their
> knees knocking, they're either braver than most or else just
> silly."
>
> "Then he isn't safe?" said Lucy.

"Safe?" said Mr. Beaver, "don't you hear what Mrs. Beaver tells you? Who said anything about safe? 'Course he isn't safe. But he's good. He's the King, I tell you."[33]

The LORD Almighty, like Aslan, is no safe or manageable King. In fact, he can be very curious. *"Who has known the mind of the Lord?"* (Romans 11:34) Can any brave soul really claim to have the right to answer that query in the affirmative? The Bible loves the fine art of the rhetorical.

In Genesis, God broods lovingly over his creation; his very word, breath, and touch carefully and passionately involved. This moment has percolated for all eternity. It is planned, purposeful, and pre-destined. Then, as quickly as it was brought to order and meaning, it surprisingly unravels and speeds rapidly toward chaos. All that brewing and brooding seems to have gone for naught as the wonder of creation is invaded by the burden of sin via one fruit and a single catastrophic act of disobedience.

The gift of life comes bearing the possibility of death. Within the garden of God's delight, there is the paradox of decay. We are made in the image of God, yet freed in our wills to reject that image outright. We are profoundly aware of our creature-status, yet freed to worship ourselves and the making of our own hands if we so determine. We are made for relationship, to find our deepest fulfillment, not alone but alongside another, and yet that place of intimacy, shared strength, and help has the potential to be the locale of the most heart-wrenching agony and abandonment. We are made to participate in God's work, yet freed to carelessly frit away the time, resources, privileges, and opportunities we have been given. What is beautiful can just as quickly become ugly. What has God started? And why does he let this all go on?

As God's revelation of himself intersects with the human story in Scripture, we find numerous times where the Ancient of Days proves he will not be tamed, boxed, or systematized. He is totally consistent and straight as an arrow, and then shockingly and unexpectedly almost schizophrenic. He says if we eat that fruit we will surely die, then allows the descendents of Adam to live for hundreds of years. He says

---

[33] C.S. Lewis, *The Lion, the Witch, and the Wardrobe,* 75.

he will destroy the race and not endure us, then hints at eternal life. He promises to protect our feet from striking even a stone, then leads us through valleys in the shadow of death. He tells us he will act, then asks us to wait. He says we must pay for our own sin, then sends his Son to pay what we owe. He says the Son must die, then raises him from the grave. He does what he says, then turns the table and does what he said he'd do in a way we never saw coming. There are moments we might wonder if he's misplaced the blueprint and is just making it up as he goes along.

To know this God is to be left awed and confused. He is odd, at least from our finite perspective. To trust this God most definitely takes faith. Reason and experience alone will not suffice, for he seems occasionally irrational and our experience of him is not always pure pleasure. To romp with this God is, once more as Lucy says in *The Lion, the Witch, and the Wardrobe*, to be unsure "whether it was more like playing with a thunderstorm or playing with a kitten."[34]

All these strange ways can, if our eyes are too shrouded by self and the temporal, lead us to miss the most fantastic point of all: this is most wonderfully God! He is who he is! He will be what and who he will be. He is "I AM," as he told Moses (Exodus 3:14), and then freely goes on to prove that what "I AM" means will be revealed and determined by him and not us. We are only asked to trust him and know him.

Despite his wildness, however, he continually proves himself good. He is compassionate, just, patient, and he acts on behalf of those who need it—even when it appears he is indifferent or far too long in coming. He is God. And this means that faith in he who is unseen is one grand adventure and no static, predictable liturgy reserved for Sunday mornings. His unpredictable wildness is somehow filled with a mysterious and glorious plan. Faith is the adventure of wagering our lives on the blessed assurance that every time this God speaks and acts, even when at first blush it seems contradictory, he can be trusted because there is something gloriously good afoot.

Faith, says Hebrews, is being sure of what we hope for and certain of what we do not see (Hebrews 11:1). Nonetheless, faith, if it is true faith, thrusts itself in the adventure of understanding just what it is

---

[34] Ibid., *The Lion, The Witch, and the Wardrobe*, 148-49.

God is up to. The sheer joy of faith is knowing *God* and his invitation to discover his hide and seek ways. Faith is a journey into the mysterious, certain future of God. Faith is an adventure in keeping up with God and his wild plan to redeem, save, and transform the world. Faith saves us from the mundane and invites us into the eternal.

At the heart of this great adventure of abandoned faith is a startling hope—God is for us! (Romans 8:31f).

The good news of the Christian Gospel is that God does not need to be appeased. We do not need to earn his favour or somehow make him like us. No, God is actively and wildly at work revealing himself to be on our side. God loves people and hates what destroys us. However, given that his ways are so untamed and occasionally outrageously unpredictable, many interpret his movements of grace as grand acts of punishment and violence by a deity who barely puts up with us and would rather not have to endure us at all. Oswald Chambers reveals our blindness, "Tis because I am so mean, Thy ways so oft look mean to me." We assume God is like us—let us be thankful he is not so tamed and predictable as we.

Both the Old Testament and New Testament reveal a God wildly on the side of humanity. Through the prophet Ezekiel, the LORD responds to the challenges and accusations of people saying he is unfair and unjust (Ezekiel 18). The law of karma that human beings so love, that we get what we deserve and must even pay off the crimes and sins of the generations above us, was being reframed by God. Though tainted and shaped by the mistakes of others, we, each of us individually, are responsible before God. People, as the LORD reminded Jonah, are his priority—"*all souls are mine*" (Ezekiel 18:4). When we take into our hands whom God is for and who he is against, we are out of our league. We are responsible for our own sin and God is for sinners. God's great longing is for people to realize he is for them: "*Have I any pleasure in the death of the wicked, declares the LORD God, and not rather that he should turn from his way and live?*" (Ezekiel 18:23)

This theme is echoed in the New Testament. Not only does God unilaterally declare he is for us by identifying with us in the Son, but

Peter the disciple of Jesus, who denied him only to realize that God is still on his side (John 21), declares, *"But do not overlook this one fact, beloved, that with the Lord one day is as a thousand years, and a thousand years as one day. The Lord is not slow to fulfill his promise as some count slowness, but is patient toward you, not wishing that any should perish, but that all should reach repentance"* (2 Peter 3:8-9). God's ways seem odd; his watch is broken. He has an eternal timeline that is shaped, undergirded and guided by his incredible desire to be for and with people.

A missional Kingdom culture is shaped by this outstanding realization. A missional people will be awake to understand the times because this wild God is at work for people right here and right now. Our conviction truly is that, despite all appearances, God does not change and he knows what he is doing. He is who he is and will be what he will be for his glory and our good. He will never change—but the times do. And so Christians must be wise, awake, and students of their age. To know God is to be sure without a shadow of a doubt that he is somehow patiently and purposefully on mission in our times, in our context, even in our confusion. Since we exist for the world our Lord came to save, we must know the times to know our place, our voice, and our appropriate action when this far from tame Lion pounces.

Two biblical stories from the life of the people of Israel take us further into the missional Kingdom declaration "We exist for the world our Lord came to save."

The first comes in the uncertain days following the death of Saul, the first King of Israel. The people, having settled in the Promised Land after exodus, wilderness wanderings, and a lengthy period of settling new territories, bellyache for a king. When faith is no longer an adventure, we lose the plot. "Everyone else has a king, why can't we?" is their cry (1 Samuel 8:6-9). Eventually, in one of his confusing ways, God concedes and grants the desires of their national heart and Saul is anointed the first royal.

Saul proves to be very human. He has moments of brilliance and moments of colossal blundering. Interestingly, his blunders are rarely obvious and could even be seen as marks of quality leadership. God is not as easily deceived as we. The King wins battles and performs the sacrifices God asks, brilliant in our eyes, but these are blunders because his heart is out of sorts and his apparent obedience is really rebellion in sheep's clothing (1 Samuel 15). God rejects Saul, whom *he* initially called, as his king.

In search of a new head to crown, and perhaps a national saviour, the prophet Samuel goes to the town of Bethlehem and the family of a man named Jesse (1 Samuel 16). There he anoints David, the most unlikely boy in the clan—again God surprises us—as the next king. However, Saul is still on the throne and it is several years, a felled giant, a few harrowing near death experiences, and a civil war before David actually finds himself even remotely near the throne (1 Samuel 17-31).

This is maddeningly confusing. It is a conundrum not only for David, who must surely have wondered if God ever really meant that little anointing ceremony in the family pasture, but also for the nation. God rejected Saul and then lets him reign until he falls on his own sword years later. By then the man has descendants, allies, and a bureaucratic system in place designed to protect his lineage and power. But David was anointed by Samuel as the next king. What's up? Where to now?

Slowly, the messy politics of Israel begin to play out. David's tribal clan rally to their own and declare him king (2 Samuel 2). Civil war erupts and a generation worth of alliances is tested. Possible heirs from Saul's clan rise up and are defeated. Is there no easier way? Has the LORD not already decided this? Why is he allowing this madness and insanity to continue?

Eventually more and more Israelites begin to see what has been there all along. The twelve tribes come one by one, including Saul's tribe of Benjamin (1 Chronicles 12:29), to hand the kingdom over to David. In many ways, this act of uniting the nation under David is a conscious recognition of what their unchanging God had been doing all along. The Lord seems exceedingly patient as he waits for us to catch up to him. God had a purpose, it was somehow linked to David, and thus the great wisdom of the chiefs of the tribe of Issachar under-stood the times and knew what Israel was supposed to do (1 Chronicles 12:32).

There is a wonderful oddness about this tribe in the list of those who came to make David king in 1 Chronicles 12. Whereas the other tribes are numbered by their warriors, soldiers, and armed men, Issachar is different. In contrast, Issachar is led by two hundred chiefs, family heads, who bring all their relatives along. For Issachar, this move to submit to the rule of David is not solely military; it is a complete and total coming over of a whole people. God was at work, they understood the confusing times, knew what Israel had to do, and they did it together.

This move of faith was rewarded. David would be promised a kingdom that would never end (2 Samuel 7) and one that was intended to bless not just the people of Israel, but all nations (2 Samuel 22:44-51; Isaiah 11:1-9). Of course, the chiefs of Issachar didn't know how it would all turn out. They only knew God—the unchanging, sovereign King—was not confounded by, but somehow mysteriously at work in, the changing times. A missional Kingdom people understand the times and jump on board when God is moving.

The story of David is all well and good, but God had clearly spoken in those early days of Israel's story. God picked David. God spoke through Samuel. There were clear benchmarks of God's intentions set up along the way. What do we do when the times are not so clear?

Eventually, David died and his son Solomon succeeded him as king. Thereafter, a long stretch of good and bad rulers filled the annals of Jewish history. In time, the regrettable consequences of the rejection of God's commands and the life of faith resulted in the people of God dividing into two separate nations, Israel (ten northern tribes who rejected David's line) and Judah (two southern tribes, Judah and Benjamin, loyal to David's heirs). Further along, both nations were individually overrun by defeat and swept into captivity by Assyria (Israel, in 722 BC) and Babylon (Judah, in 586 BC). Thus was ushered in a new season of confusion.

Jeremiah the prophet instructed the Jews in Babylon to make themselves at home. Though God would act once again and return them to the Promised Land, it would not happen overnight—surprise,

surprise (Jeremiah 29:4-14)! So, they settled in. They didn't really have any other choice. Years passed as a new generation was born and raised in a Babylonian world. Eventually, Babylon itself crumbled and the Persians became the Middle East's Superpower *du jour*. A lot of water had gone down the Euphrates and God had not yet acted. Where was he with his strange ways?

And then the Persian King Xerxes, having deposed his Queen, Vashti, for her act of insubordination, searches his Empire for a suitable replacement (Esther 1). Forced into the king's harem and this ancient beauty pageant was Hadassah, an orphaned young woman who had been raised by her older cousin, Mordecai. Hadassah, who went by the Gentile name of Esther to hide her true identity, captured the heart of Xerxes and was crowned Queen of Persia. Imagine that!

More time slips by and Haman, the highest noble in the land, develops a Hitlerian scheme to rid the kingdom of Jews because Mordecai would not pay him homage and stroke his fragile ego. Haman manages to secure Xerxes' approval for this genocide and a day is set aside for this most gruesome and menacing of acts.

Unbeknown to Xerxes, however, his Queen is on the hit list, too.

With the public announcement of the demise of the Jews making headlines, Mordecai approaches Esther, pleading with her to intervene on behalf of her people. She is unsure, knowing she risks much to approach the king uninvited, even as his wife. In response to her hesitancy, Mordecai sends his infamous words,

> *Do not think to yourself that in the king's palace you will escape any more than all the other Jews. For if you keep silent at this time, relief and deliverance will rise for the Jews from another place, but you and your father's house will perish. And who knows whether you have not come to the kingdom for such a time as this?*

ESTHER 4:13-14

Esther does the courageous thing, her bravery and faith are rewarded, genocide is averted, and the Jews survive to be the people through whom God will bless the nations with a Saviour.

117

There is one glaring and fascinating omission in the whole story of Esther: God is not mentioned, not even once. Despite the clear providential moves of his hand—Esther elevated to royalty being just one in a series of not-so-coincidental acts—God gets no credit. And yet Mordecai clearly understands the times and knows something about God even when he seems conspicuously absent. He knows God is for his people. He knows God delivers. He knows God directs circumstances and seasons. He knows it is not happenstance that raised an orphaned Jewish girl to Queen of a great world Empire. The times require steps of faith be taken and the unseen, unchanging God has his ducks in a row for such a time as this.

It is fascinating that the Bible, a collection of books and letters written over centuries declared authoritative for faith and life because of what they reveal *about* God, includes a book that seemingly excludes him. I find this entirely encouraging.

A missional Kingdom culture exists for the world our Lord came to save, even when he appears absent. Awake to the times, students of the age, season, and peoples to which we have been called, the missional community is free to walk in faith during the most confounding of eras. God is never absent. He never changes, even amidst change ups. He is for people. He is on our side. He is seeking the good of all nations and peoples. We are invited into the faith-filled adventure of joining his mysterious ways. For such a time as this, we have been called. Our task is to understand the times and know what our God would have us do.

I remember two torturous experiences as a boy disinterested in chivalry, propriety, and all things "girly." The first was being forced to watch *The Sound of Music* every Christmas by my mother and aunt, until my cousin and I were bold enough to mutiny. Julie Andrews with a guitar on an alpine hillside may be soothing to some, but it gives me the heebie-jeebies. The second was being forced to watch the marriage of Charles, Prince of Wales, and Diana Spencer, who was simply and affectionately known as "Lady Di." I recall being dragged out of bed to watch history happen in all its pomp and circumstance as those two entered not-so wedded bliss.

Several years later, on September 1, 1997, my own wife and I stood on a pier in British Columbia awaiting departure from Vancouver Island for the mainland. We had been camping in the pouring rain for a week—a good test for our young marriage which I think Jen passed more gracefully than I—and had been unaware of current events. As we waited to board the ferry, I picked up a newspaper and read, even to my anti-royal shock, that Lady Diana, Princess of Wales, had been killed during the night in a single car crash in a Paris tunnel. Time seemed to stand still in those days as a powerful grief gripped whole nations and seemed to baffle the royal family at Windsor Castle. Caught up in the wave of popular emotion, and having most likely gone temporarily insane even I recorded the funeral.

In 2006, *The Queen*, a movie giving an interpretation of those tenuous days inside the British hierarchy, was released. It gained critical acclaim and won an Oscar for actress Helen Mirren's performance as Queen Elizabeth II. What struck me as I watched this film, to my mother's delight, was the way an ancient, staid institution grappled with the realities of a changing world.

Diana had rocked the monarchy. She was beautiful, photogenic, likeable, appealing to the masses, and unpredictable. She made Prince Charles look good, then in divorce made him look bad. For me, the ironically intrigued royal dissenter, the most telling statement in the film took place in a conversation during a garden stroll between Elizabeth and the Queen Mother in the days following Diana's death. The Queen, seeking to understand the bizarre grief of the masses, comparing it to times past, wrestling with unheard of demands made by her people and the Prime Minister regarding her response, says, "Something's happened ... there's been a change ... some shift in values." She can't quite put her finger on it. This new land she finds herself leading is just beyond her grasp. She doesn't understand the times and yet must lead in them.

What must it be like to be a ruler for whom the changing times are a mystery?

◆◆◆◆◆

A missional Kingdom culture that declares "We exist for the world our Lord came to save!" finds itself in the same world as Queen Elizabeth II. The Christendom world that shaped the culture and experiences of many Christians and non-Christians alike is gone. Not just eroded, not just staggering like a boxer who might yet recover and win in some Rocky-esque flash of glory, but gone. Oh, there are still vestiges and remnants yet to be seen, increasingly as tourists, and there will be for some time. But as that which gives shape to the values and direction of a culture, Christendom is dead.

We know this, at least by observation and experience, but we don't want to admit it. And we don't know what to do about it. We are, like the Jews in exile, in a foreign land. Generation X writer Richard Tiplady says about postmodernism: "The word has no meaning. Use it as often as you can."[35] Something's happened ... there's been a change ... some shift in values, and we all feel it, see it, live it, but can barely describe it.

We're in good company. It is not only Christians who are confused by where we're we find ourselves. Philosopher Ludwig Wittgenstein sums up the disappointment of a previous age and the hunger of these new times: "We feel that even when all possible scientific questions have been answered, the problems of life remain completely untouched."[36] This also implies that the church, having been so wrapped up in institutional, scientific, and rational modernity, has provided no alternative answer or story for the searching soul to cling to. In fact, it has been argued that the church of the Enlightenment period (early 1700s and on) was really the seedbed and incubator of the very modernity that irreversibly crippled her influence.[37]

---

[35] Creps, *Off-Road Disciplines*, 28. Tiplady's book, *Postmission,* is a helpful discussion of the way Generation X (born around 1964 to about 1980) views mission to their world.

[36] Quoted in Brian Appleyard, *Understanding the Present,* 15.

[37] For a very involved and intriguing argument along these lines, check out John Milbank's *Theology and Social Theory*. It will stretch your intellect and put you to sleep, occasionally at the same time. Milbank argues that what spun out of the theology of Christendom/Enlightenment was an unbiblical social theory that is, in reality, a new religion in and of itself. The problem is that many western Christians, and some entire denominations, swallowed this new religion *carte blanche* and then passed it on as the real thing. The decline of genuine Christian influence on society since this experiment is the fruit of its true roots.

The change and shift in values actually means the culture, in abandoning all things joined to the modern world including the church, no longer looks to the church for answers to anything outside of "Will you marry us?" or "Will you bury us?" Even our answers to those questions are increasingly irrelevant. The church, as an institution, has been thrown out with the bath water. Tim Bednar points out, "The problem is that most postmoderns would rather die than have the church (or God) meet their needs."[38]

In the often vigorous culture debate over same-sex marriage in Canada in 2004, a letter to the editor in one national newspaper boldly proclaimed, "The charter of rights trumps the Bible." Such a statement would have been unthinkable a generation earlier. Individual rights are *the* source of postmodern authority. Other authorities like the Bible may have personal value, but have no place in the public square. Our culture echoes the words of the tragic figure Bazarov in Ivan Turgenev's 1862 novel *Fathers and Sons*, which reads like a current generational commentary: "I only gaze up to heaven when I want to sneeze."

It's not, however, that people no longer search for answers to the more mysterious and spiritual questions of life. Such longing is actually immense. They hunger and thirst and are filling the void with just about everything conceivable.

There is, in our times, a rich and warm embrace of all things spiritual. You can see it everywhere from the marketplace[39] to the political arena. For example, the swearing in ceremony of Paul Martin as Prime Minister of Canada in 2004 included a native incense ceremony, a statement that not only indicated a necessary inclusion of aboriginals in places of influence, but also said spirituality and politics are not as divorced as modernity tries to convince us. Perhaps not so surprisingly, the only message that seems still ostracized is that of Christians—our culture shutters at the thought of a return to the Church/State marriage that got us into this mess in the first place. They may be wiser than we, who believe all our ills would be healed if

[38] Quoted from Bednar's article, "Why Rick Warren and the Purpose Driven Church Model Will Not Evangelize the 21st Century," in Creps, *Off-Road Disciplines,* 37
[39] Even as I write this, I am watching a television commercial that uses a Jesus-type figure to sell cars.

only the church ran the government. That's never gone very well, and as a rule results in the abdication of the Church's unique call.[40]

So the challenge facing the church on mission with God in this befuddling age is whether we will have the courage and ability to unlearn what we have known and be a missional Kingdom culture that understands the times and responds accordingly.

To complicate matters, there is a renewed and passionate "evan-gelical" atheism gaining momentum these days.[41] In many ways, it is the rehashing of old arguments, but nonetheless it is receiving a wide and popular audience. This new "God is not good" movement will most likely, however, come up against the same reality the church is already keenly aware of in western culture: despite our interest in all things spiritual—and atheism itself can't avoid being brought into the very spiritual realm they rail against—there is, at the end of the day, an apathetic indifference to just about everything.

While you can draw a crowd and elicit incredible response in the face of tragedy, disaster, and need—Diana's funeral being one example[42]—these really seem to be over-exaggerated blips of life on the heart monitor of a comatose contemporary society. We generally don't get upset about all that much when it boils right down to it. By and large, we sit watching our televisions, baffled by those who are all hot and bothered. We can't seem to commit to anything that might remotely involve personal sacrifice, though we indulge ourselves on great stories of personal sacrifice at theatres and our mammoth home entertainment centers. We love this stuff, so long as it amuses us.

The values truly have shifted. We are on a spiritual search. We want a cause; we want to feel alive, but find ourselves in the Land of Me—the sovereign dominion of the individual. Even we who are kings

---

[40] Karl Barth in *Community, State and Church: Three Essays* declared, "The Church would be denying its own existence if it wished to become a State and to establish law by force, when it should be preaching justification." Stanley Hauerwas says in *Resident Aliens* that "the overriding political task of the church is to be the community of the cross."

[41] Richard Dawkins, *The God Delusion* (2006). At Dawkins' website, you can by t-shirts bearing the "scarlet letter," *A* for atheism, to proclaim your "faith" proudly. Michael Onfray's *The Atheist Manifesto* (2007) and Christopher Hitchens' *God is not Great: How Religion Poisons Everything* (2007) are examples of this new wave.

[42] As well as the 2005 tsunami in South Asia and, even more recently, the earthquakes in Pakistan and China.

and queens of self don't fully know what that means; we just find our-selves there, sold and told to like it.

Western society is home of a million little "me's." Of course this is not entirely new, but never before has this become the wholesale and mass doctrine of an entire culture. Never before have we been able to broadcast our domain so freely and unabashedly, thanks to the world wide web. We are, as Charles Taylor points out, the first society in history where rejection of God and the spiritual for a purely self-sufficient humanism—a worldview in which human beings answer only to themselves—is a completely feasible and available option.[43]

From the midst of this strange mix of immense hunger, confusion, individualism, loneliness, intellectualism, and consumerism, Christians are a saved and called out then sent back to by God. The presence of the Church in mystifying times is a window into another world. The challenge facing the church on mission with God in this befuddling age is whether we will have the courage and ability to unlearn what we have known. Will we *be* a missional Kingdom culture that lives with a determination to understand the times, since we exist for this world that God continues to be for? He is on mission. We will see him if we look carefully and walk and act by faith. But how do we do it?

First, as a missional Kingdom culture that understands the times, we center on Jesus the Lord of history and King of Kings. The church has always faced great cultural challenges—from the Roman Empire in Europe to the rise if Islam in North Africa to Maoist China—and she still remains and even thrives. Why? Because of Jesus who must reign (1 Corinthians 15:25-28) and for whom all things were created and through whom all things will be reconciled (Colossians 1:15-20). Our God, who confounds us from time to time with his ways and what he will endure, has never changed on this: Christ shall have dominion. He may not be a tame lion, but he is *the* King nonetheless. Therefore, a missional Kingdom culture is free to live fearlessly and

---

[43] Charles Taylor, *A Secular Age,* 18. Taylor, one of the most distinguished philosophers of social science in the world, notes that this current secular and postmodern age is the fruit of a "Modern civilization (that) cannot but bring about a 'death of God.'"

confidently in any age—even suffering if given the privilege—for the name of Jesus. He will ride in as King of Kings (Revelation 19:11-16) and even such a time as this is headed in that direction. At the end of the day, our prophetic task is that of John the Baptist—we point away from ourselves and to Jesus Christ.

Second, as a missional Kingdom culture that understands the times, we embrace our true call. Since we exist for the world our Lord came to save, we dream with Stanley Hauerwas: "We would like a church that again asserts that God, not nations rules the world, that the boundaries of God's kingdom transcend those of Caesar, and that the main political task of the church is the transformation of people who see clearly the cost of discipleship and are willing to pay the price."[44] Like Esther, we accept that we have been called for such a time as this and then engage the one task given us by Jesus the King: to make disciples who will know their true identity as blessed and blessing sons and daughters of the Father. The task of understanding our times is for this purpose—to know how to relate to people, to know how they think, love, fear, and thirst—not merely for the sport of cultural voyeurism. We are not like Jonah, sitting on a hillside beneath a comfortable vine hoping for the destruction of what lies below. We are engaged students of our times for the purpose of life transformation in the lives of people God loves. With Esther, this takes great courage, but if we don't rise up with courage and faith, people will perish and that is not our King's desire.

Third, as a missional Kingdom culture that understands the times, we practice the disciplines of learning and unlearning. Too many churches are engaging the culture as if nothing much has changed since Martin Luther nailed his 95 theses to the Wittenberg door and Menno Simons trudged through the Dutch lowlands baptizing and organizing potlucks.

The church ought to be the learning organism *par excellence*. This means we hang on with unwavering conviction to that which has sustained the church, learn well the adjustments previous generations have made, but equally hold with open hands and quickly dispense with that which has run its course. Since our wild God seems to work

[44] Stanley Hauerwas, *Resident Aliens*, 48.

with such patient purpose within the chaos and disorder of this world for the sake of people, his creation, and salvation, surely we are free to rejoice, "We've never done it this way before!"

Where there is faithfulness to the Apostolic message that has been passed down, it seems God permits great freedom of expression. A learning organism will reflect the wildness of the untamed God it loves and willingly embrace the joy of understanding its times, changing course when necessary so that it can be for people as God is. Faith is the adventure of joining God in mission, not just nodding at a creed and then nodding off.

The Spirit is a creative force. A learning people on mission with God will welcome fresh winds and not be distracted by inconsequential trivialities. Learning organizations, led by the Spirit's fresh air, are wise to the Enemy's schemes. The Devil distracts by making mountains out of that which the Bible gives no command—styles of music, types of sermons, buildings and architecture, and even when we should meet. Search as we may, we will be straining out a gnat to find verses to build our churchianity around. Dallas Willard writes,

> Now you might ask yourself, Why does the New Testament say nothing about all those matters to which the usual congregation today devotes almost all its thoughts and efforts? Answer: Because those matters are not primary and will take care of themselves with little attention whenever what is primary is appropriately cared for. Pay attention to the "principles and absolutes" of the New Testament church and, one might suppose, everything else will fall into place—in large part because "everything else" really doesn't matter much one way or the other.[45]

The learning church on mission with God has eyes rightly focused Biblically and corporately—we are about the mission God is on and everything else is just details.

---

[45] Dallas Willard, *Renovation of the Heart*, 236.

The discipline of learning comes through vital relationships across generational, ethnic, and cultural boundaries. These relationships are best face to face and life-on-life, but can also extend to the books and newspapers we read (you can have great relationships with history and other cultures this way), the media we pay attention to (movies tell us a lot about what is thought and believed), and events and trends that dominate the culture we inhabit (for instance, the emergence of ultimate fighting as a mainstream sport tells us a lot about who we are becoming—or maybe already are).

The discipline of unlearning requires that we ask two questions: "Why?"[46] and "If we were starting this from scratch today, is this how we'd do it?"

A child learns by asking "Why?" and it seems grownups *unlearn* through a willingness to continue using this same simple question. Why do we stop asking why? Our churches, if they are to be missional and understand the times, can be primed to unlearn unhelpful patterns and practices by frequently applying this simple word. Couple that with the second question above and we are primed for a freshness of the Spirit in the context we call home. To learn and unlearn, we must love God and the world. G.K. Chesterton says, "We must be fond of this world, even in order to change it ... we must be fond of another world in order to have something to change it to."[47] This loving fondness and asking good questions will keep us learning and unlearning.

Unlearning, however, requires not simply accumulating information or proudly naming what is wrong, but immediately engaging by taking steps to respond redemptively to what we have understood about our times. We unlearn by asking and learn by doing.

Our postmodern tendency to deconstruct everything too seldom results in building anything hopeful. I confess that my generation is very prone to criticism and deconstruction, but hesitant to actually foster any practical steps in a different yet faithful direction, because that requires commitment—and we're too busy, distracted, and cult-

---

[46] My friend and colleague Tim Doherty has inserted this often unwelcome and disconcerting question at the center of our life at Kingsfield. I am grateful for what he has helped me learn and unlearn by it.

[47] G.K. Chesteron, *Orthodoxy*, 105.

ured for that. Unlearning is useless, and unbiblical, if it doesn't erupt in the creativity of Spirit borne from our rootedness in the principles and absolutes of our wild God.

Fourth, as a missional Kingdom culture that understands the times, we live a counter-cultural ethic. We will develop this in much more depth in the next chapter, but for now it is crucial to note that if we understand the times at all, we will be awakened to the enormous impact the church has had, and will have again, when Christians actually live in the power of the Spirit what Jesus taught. God is wild and he creates a people that appear equally as wild in a world that is dazed, confused, and divided. If the ache and decay in our culture is "normal," then our great joy ought to be our abnormality! God's people, like the Israel David and Esther led and the community Herrnhut became, ought to be extraordinarily peculiar—and that's a good thing. A missional Kingdom culture will live as the tangible evidence and presence of a different reality in a world brought to ask, "Why do they live like that?" To which it will be our great joy to reply, "It's because we exist for the world our Lord came to save!"

UPON FURTHER REVIEW...

- Consider times when you and/or your church experienced the wildness and untamed reality of the Living God. When has he surprised you and what did that awaken?

- How would you describe the times in which you live? What is a typical person in your community like? How have the times shaped you, even unknowingly?

- What must you and your faith community learn and unlearn as you seek to grow disciples in such a time as this? How will you do this? And will you ask, "Why?"

A Kingdom Culture That
Is Wildly Different

It shall not be so among you.

JESUS (MATTHEW 20:26)

Our duty is clear: to be courageous in the cause of love and in the hate of hate.

QUAKER LETTER TO THE BRITISH EMPIRE (1914)

When we read the sacrificial feats of saints like the Moravians, we can be left flustered, chastised, and disappointed. Lives like those seem too good and holy to be true. How can we ever begin to match such exploits? Do we need to? Keenly aware of just how sporadic our discipleship is and how fancy our dance between the flesh and the Spirit is, we can hide behind the reasonable conclusion that such an extraordinary life is not possible for us.

Once we begin to think about this corporately, and not only individually, it becomes even more troubling. It's one thing for me as an individual to be captured by some noble ideal and throw my life into it in one grand blind leap. But what are the odds, really, that a whole people—a gathering of twenty, seventy-five, or one thousand five hundred and sixteen—can actually be united enough to live with the counter-cultural significance of the people we read about in history books? We know our fellowships. We know what we're really like.

How quickly we forget that Zinzendorf was a law school dropout, Dober a potter, and Nitschmann a builder. Even if we think carefully about the Biblical characters we have been living with, we discover that David was the runt of the litter and shepherd to boot. Esther was an orphan in captivity. Peter was a fisherman with a tendency to put his foot in his mouth. Matthew collected taxes. Mary Magdalene was reportedly a sex trade worker. And, most extraordinary of all, when God the Father sends his Son into the world to bear our flesh, he is raised in a village of dubious reputation, Nazareth, where he is trained as a carpenter.

How short our memories are in recalling that the Moravians were as diverse and common a people as you can imagine. This is a consistent quality of most renewal movements that change the course of history. The band of Jesus' disciples was almost comically miscellaneous in nature. Fishermen, a tax collector, a zealot, momma's boys, two sets of brothers, a money-launderer who actively worked to betray him—for heaven's sake! If this Messiah-thing hadn't worked out, Jesus could have written a bestseller on conflict resolution or earned a doctorate for the study of dysfunctional group dynamics. Jesus' selection of his closest companions—chosen after serious prayer no less (Luke 6:12-16)—is perhaps one of the most wildly dangerous decisions he made. Pinning the hopes of God's mission on this eclectic crew is kind of like leaving the keys of the fireworks factory to a gaggle of ten-year-old boys. It had the potential to blow up real good. If this plan works, it will be nothing short of the true Hail Mary.

It would appear God intends the infiltration of his Kingdom on earth to be a very covert operation. It is best started where no one expects and among those most likely to fail. If you and I planned his arrival, we'd have looked to Jerusalem, Rome, or Athens, even some Far Eastern civilization. Even more likely, we'd have delayed his arrival until a New York, Paris, or Tokyo was ready.

If we were choosing whom to call as the champions of the movement, we'd have looked in palaces, universities, and among the respected classes. But, of course, we're too tame and uncreative. God chooses to do things backwards, unsuspectingly, invisibly, against all odds; like yeast working through dough, like the smallest seed becoming a tree. Not only does this fit the wild ways of God, but it proves his transforming power—if he can change the world from Nazareth and use fishers and orphans, uniting zealots and tax collectors in the same cause, he can use anyone from anywhere. Any mosaic of saints is laden with Kingdom potential!

The greatest witnesses of the coming Kingdom are seen in any community on the planet where people of incredible variety are committed to living life together under the Lordship of Jesus. The Church is, by its very nature, a stupendous miracle: a declaration that God is real and doing something extraordinary! The Church is the witness that the Kingdom has and is coming!

As a pastor, I have the privilege of serving such an incredible wonder week after week. I marvel at how amazing it is that anyone shows up on Sunday mornings when we gather. What is it that draws these people together and causes them to serve one another? Arguing that it is family or tradition just doesn't hold water. There really is no such thing as a "family church." In fact, many older parents these days are realizing that just because their children were raised in the faith is no slam dunk that they will continue to embrace it. An honest look at our church families will reveal that determining who will walk in the footsteps of Jesus in the long run is no predictable science and does not always follow family trees. Church photo directories illustrate this truth; the faces change in more ways than one as time moves along.

Furthermore, tradition might contribute to the Christmas and Easter rush, but as the glue that sustains a movement, tradition is being shown in these postmodern days to be about as useless as trying to harness a Clydesdale with quilting thread. Tradition creates warm fuzzies, stirs some nostalgic longing, or satisfies some genealogical tourism, but it does not explain the church. Tradition, at its best, preserves what has worth and value, but it is a worth and value that, if not caught and lived by each subsequent generation, becomes powerless. It becomes the equivalent of people gathering at Gettysburg to re-enact history. Historian Jarislav Pelikan had it right when he noted, "Tradition is the living faith of the dead. Traditionalism is the dead faith of the living."

Leaders also have their place, but they come and go because their humanity will disappoint. Hitching our hopes to a leader in these consumerist days is a mass exodus just waiting to happen. There will always be another celebrity to run to. We are a culture constantly on the prowl for the next great product—even religious product—to satisfy us. Thinking some human leader will be our panacea produces a spiritual paparazzi. We chase the next new fad until we're tired of it and move on again. Whom we love today may become our whipping post tomorrow.

Blood lines, tradition, and leaders just don't explain what we see in this phenomenon known as the church. Every week, I look out and see a people who would not even know each other, who would never gather meaningfully, who would never do good together, were it not for the wonder of Jesus and his ability to form *communitas* where there is none. *Ex nihilo*—out of nothing—God creates a people who are the salt of the earth and the light of the world. This is the glory of his wild ways. The church in every community, no matter what the size, is an astounding miracle!

With this in mind, we can set aside the foolish notion that somehow it is our relevance that defines our capacity to be a church on mission with God. Instead, we must live a *holy irrelevance*. As a missional Kingdom culture that exists for the world our Lord came to save, we unashamedly embrace the call to be wildly different. With our wild God, we are *for* the world and equally find ourselves *against* it, even hated by it. How can this be?

The marvellous myriad of people Jesus called into his inner circle entered a three-year program in postmodern deconstruction—they just didn't call it that. Everything they assumed to be current and relevant about life required careful deconstruction, followed by determined reconstruction on the person of Jesus, the simple carpenter from Nazareth.

In a world tamed and spoiled by sin, Jesus knows that to sustain a movement a people must be discipled, taught to actually live, as the embodiment of a different world. As he sits to teach his disciples on a hillside in Matthew 5-7, he goes to great lengths describing a people extraordinarily and wildly different than any other people previously known. The poor in spirit, the mourning, the meek, the hungry, the merciful, the pure, the peacemakers, the persecuted because of him— these are the blessed. Happy are the irrelevant.

Six times he will say, "You have heard that it was said," only to add his own "But I say to you." What we have been told by our culture has been lacking, incomplete, and too tame. The religious world's description of the way things are and should be is sorely incomplete.

131

The people God forms, the people Jesus comes to redeem and recreate, is a wildly different description of life as we know it on the planet. The Sermon on the Mount defines a holy nation. The Kingdom of God is seen in communities of holy irrelevance.

This emphasis is no more strongly declared by Jesus than when he is brought into a quarrel among his disciples over who gets the seats of power in his Kingdom (Matthew 20:20-28). The two momma's boys, James and John, desire to sit on the right and left of Jesus on his throne. At the heart of their desire is an understanding of God's Kingdom that is shaped by the culture in which they live. Jesus responds by explaining that in this world everyone clamours for a little plot of real estate where they can "lord it over" others. Everyone thinks that if they could just be in power they'd know best, do best, and be free.

With great force, Jesus redefines and reframes what life is like in his Kingdom: "It shall not be so among you." Jesus' Kingdom will not be like the kingdoms of this world, no matter how big or small. He has not come to create a parallel political regime nor the ideal theocracy. He has come to create a whole new world from the one we have assumed. *"But whoever would be great among you must be your servant, and whoever would be first among you must be your slave, even as the Son of Man came not to be served but to serve, and to give his life as a ransom for many"* (Matthew 20:26-28). The culture in Jesus' Kingdom is wildly different than anything we've ever seen.

One of the primary values of the church in recent times has been the hunt for relevance. Seeing our influence wane in the broader culture, we began thinking that maybe we're just misunderstood, that maybe if we spoke a language people wanted, then maybe, just maybe, the mass exodus from the church towards the gods of consumerism and self could be stemmed. So with pure motives salted nicely by our need to be liked and feel good, many churches threw all their eggs into the basket of parroting the culture at every turn. Music, the Bible, our programs—youth ministry, especially—all became like the world, with Jesus as the hip blesser of everything we can't get enough of. Again, this was noble, but sadly misguided. Why?

First of all, when the church tries to pull off being like the world to convince the world to stop being the world, the world sees through its hypocrisy. To try to convince a selfish culture to be unselfish like Jesus, by appealing to their consumerist selfishness, is a shopping mall and sitcom just waiting to happen. One wonders if our desire for relevance is more connected to a not-so-subtle fear of truly being different, of being openly identified as Jesus' disciples. The truth is that for all our investment in "relevance" in recent years, the quality and quantity of Christian discipleship has visibly gone in the opposite direction. As Michael Horton mourns, "Evangelical Christians are as likely to embrace lifestyles every bit as hedonistic, materialistic, self-centered, and sexually immoral as the world in general."[48] Convinced people will like Jesus if we cater to them, we are reaping the rewards of having consumed ourselves into a laughing stock—a reality irreverently milked for all its worth by comedians and Hollywood.

Second, we misdiagnosed the problem. The real issue facing the world is not whether they think Jesus or his band of merry women and men are relevant. Most people actually have great respect for Jesus, even in what little they know of him. But this is precisely the problem—they don't see enough of Jesus in his people. In the documentary *Super Size Me*, American school children are shown pictures of various famous people. They recognize Ronald McDonald, but not Jesus—even if the picture was the white, blue-eyed version. Without seeing the uncommon righteousness of Jesus in his people, our culture is naively unaware of the dark issue we all face: sin, that crippling disease which causes us to settle into the Land of Me, cutting us off from our neighbours, separating us from our Creator, all rooted in the hopelessness of spiritual death.

Of course, the desire to be relevant was an attempt to awaken the realization of sin in the world. Instead, by using some of the most rotten fruits of sin to do so (consumerism and selfishness), the relevance-seeking church thwarted its own message in the process. We also decided we needed to set aside hot topics like hell and judgment if we were to be heard. Unfortunately, however, the medium

---

[48] Ron Sider, *The Scandal of the Evangelical Conscience*, 17. For statistics verifying this statement, check out the various studies and surveys of George Barna (www.barna.org).

became the message and what we produced were consumers and not wildly different disciples. In many respects, we reinforced sin, giving it camouflage, and made it even more difficult to spot, rather than calling its bluff.

It should be pointed out that there are two flavours of the relevant church: the evangelical (focused primarily on saving souls with cool music and "Christianized" entertainment) and the social gospel (focused primarily on righting injustices and "Christianized" Marxism). Both believe they have found the best way to reach the culture. Both have noble goals and Kingdom objectives, but go light on or too narrowly define the real problem of sin—a problem that gets clouded by the mediums used. For the modern evangelical, sin is almost always personal and linked to bad behaviour. For the socially conscious Christian, sin is almost always systemic and linked to greed, wealth, and exploitation. Both are unbalanced and need the strength of the other in order to communicate the full depths of what the Fall has done to us and clearly declare our remedy.

Third, having misdiagnosed the problem, we misplaced the solution. Our move to transform ourselves into relevant containers of a pleasing Gospel meant we centered the life of the relevant community in the wrong place. We made our gatherings, our worship *services*, the primary place to be relevant to the world. So, in evangelical circles, we went multimedia and talked the politics of the right, and in social gospel circles, we went granola and talked the politics of the left. We thought that since the problem was really people being uncomfortable in our buildings and thinking we were out of touch, transforming our services—or abandoning them outright—would be the solution. We failed, however, to realize that the migration away from the gathered church was a spiritual problem, not a programmatic one. And so we misplaced the solution on the safe altars of our tastes and wants and consumed ourselves to death while the people we claimed this was all for golfed, did yoga, or went shopping.

In the end, this turned in upon us. Entrenched camps were set up, from social issues to music styles, and we clustered ourselves with people who liked what we liked. Rather than being a body, we became a strip mall full of competing flavour of the month preferences. When relevance is the chief value in the land of a million little me's, however, you find yourself incapable of being truly "relevant" to everyone at the same time. So churches fought and bickered over trivialities as the demons snickered. More weighty issues, and the question of whether we were following Jesus at all, were put on the back burner and left to a few prophets to remind us. Of course, we couldn't hear them amidst all the noise. The fruit of all this turned out to be money poorly spent, witness poorly wasted, social issues addressed without Gospel, and Gospel addressed without social issues. Many simply retreated to living rooms and satellite TVs, where they were sure to find the "church" they wanted, which their own community could never provide to their liking. The church became a people in self-induced captivity while the culture spun increasingly out of control.

Fourth, we had a wrong definition of relevance. Thinking that relevance meant copying and pasting the ways of the world onto the Christian Gospel, we missed that Jesus defined relevance entirely different.

Now, it must be said that speaking the language of people is hugely important. In fact, it is crucial if we understand the times. One great mark of genuine missional Kingdom movements in history has been their eager readiness and ability to make the Gospel understandable to the common person. This ability is a great gift of counter-cultural authenticity and a sign that the Spirit of God has truly penetrated who we are.

Jesus understood that God needed to be understandable. He was God *incarnate*, after all. He reframed what had once been said, he spoke in parables, and entered lives no one else would. He was unmercifully clear in his communication (which is why many traditionalists didn't get him and sought to kill him, and why the tax collectors and prostitutes flocked to him). At the same time, however, he did not allow his fledgling band to place worldly definitions and expectations on his Kingdom. His was to be an extraordinarily different Kingdom than the world had yet seen. Its relevance would be seen not in the methods and styles of his followers and their ability to parody the world—without bad language and with Birkenstocks—but in the life they lived. For Jesus, relevance is not in forms which only go skin deep; it is something we declare with our life together because of who we are as his disciples. As such, in practice, the disciples of Jesus ought to be

135

wholly different than everyone else around them, while at first blush appearing to be no different. The Church of Jesus will be a wild and extraordinary Kingdom of holy irrelevance.

In 2001, our family decided we needed to get beyond our comfort zone. Through a connection with an incredible organization that served newcomers to our area, we were put in touch with a single Muslim mom with five boys who had just arrived as refugees in Canada from Eritrea.

Jen and our only son at the time spent numerous hours helping this dear woman learn where to shop and how to adjust to strange North American ways as she and the boys lived in a two room halfway house apartment. The kids loved being together and we learned to love them immensely.

After a few weeks, we embarked on the mission to find a suitable long-term home—no small task, as you can imagine. We visited countless high rises, all with vacancies, but none would take her and her brood. It was thoroughly frustrating. I became aware, in some ways for the first time, how racist and prejudiced my culture was, especially in those post-9/11 days. Finally, we found a place in a government-subsidized townhouse in the inner city. They were thrilled.

Though they knew other Muslims from their homeland in the area, it was people from our church family who found furniture and got this family moved into their new home. We had great meals with her and, slowly and steadily, her guard dropped. We rushed to help when the landlord threatened to evict them when she missed her first rental payment. She wasn't tardy; she just didn't understand the system. And then we moved away.

Our move across the country was devastating to her. She couldn't understand why we'd go all the way to western Canada when we had so much right where we were. The goodbye was hard.

During a trip home to see family, we stopped in for a visit. She was getting used to the idea of snow. The boys were doing well in school and becoming basketball stars. Her English was improving. They were settling in quite nicely. Over tea that day—she always made tea in beautiful glass cup, she said something profound. As we talked about our times together over the years since her fearful arrival on Canadian soil from a war and a troubled story we were only barely piecing together, she said, "You have done so much for us. You have done what even our own people will not do. Why?" Our response—I couldn't think of anything else to say—was "Because it is how Jesus would want us to live."

I realized something incredible that day with our African friend in her simple apartment, the Koran open on the table so the boys could keep learning Arabic: Christians can be wildly different and we don't realize it. Perhaps we don't offer this wildness as often as we ought to.

This is the holy irrelevance I have been pointing us toward. The disciples of Jesus discover that they bring something wholly foreign to this world ruled by self and bound by human borders, blood lines, and rules of relevance.

The wild, extraordinary difference with which Christians are to live, this holy irrelevance, is not something concocted, manufactured or mass produced. It is not something we market. It is the fruit of who we are in Christ that emerges from a missional Kingdom culture centered on Jesus.

It never occurred to us that we were really all that different in standing at a Muslim mother's side. I can't claim for us some super-spirituality or the delivery of some great evangelistic shtick, but once our Christ-centered lives entered a place where he is yet a stranger, what emerged was something our friend saw that we weren't even aware of. It is a beautiful thing when the left hand is unaware what the right hand is doing (Matthew 6:3).

The Moravians did not set out to be different; they were simply captured by the person, vision, and purpose of Jesus. They found themselves unable to resist the magnetic pull to exist for the world. The whole community, including those who "stayed behind" at Herrnhut, was joined together in the task. Wherever God placed them, they were on mission with him. Every vocation was a ministry. They were wildly different. They loved and avoided exploitation. They became like others so that they could see Jesus. They rejected the notion that others had to be like them first. In a world of colonial expansion and selfish ends, the Moravians were selfless, non-territorial people of peace and truly irrelevant, and therefore holy. The powers that be deemed them expendable nuisances and even traitors. To be on the Lamb's side is treacherous and confusing. Our confused age is starving and parched for this other world to be possible, even when it hates us.

In the early days of the church, beneath the powerful thumb of the Roman Empire, the wild and extraordinary difference of Christian life stunned the pagan Romans. When catastrophic plagues took the lives of a quarter to one-third of the population between 165-260 AD, it was the life of the church in her practical love and service to humanity that stood out. Dionysius, bishop of Alexandria in North Africa (died circa 264 AD), wrote that while the Roman peoples "pushed the sufferers away and fled from their dearest," the Christians were markedly peculiar: "Most of our brother Christians showed unbounded love and loyalty; never sparing themselves and thinking only of one another. Heedless of the danger, they took charge of the sick, attending to their every need and ministering to them in Christ." Tertullian, whose writings to the Roman establishment defended and explained Christian life and convictions, declared, "It is our care of the helpless, our practice of loving kindness that brands us in the eyes of many of our opponents. 'Only look,' they say, 'look how they love one another.'"

This loving kindness, however, was not simply reserved for those within the body of Christ. Pontanius, reflecting first hand on Cyprian's instruction to the disciples he led in North Africa to care for all who were suffering, notes, "He (Cyprian) proceeds to add that there is nothing remarkable in cherishing merely our own people ... but that one might become perfect who should do something more than heathen men or publicans, one who, overcoming evil with good, and practicing merciful kindness like that of God, should love his enemies as well ... Thus good was done to all men, not merely to the household of faith." This life of wild difference made its impact. A century later when the Emperor Julian, known as the Apostate for his desire to destroy the Christianity that had swept the Empire, said, "The impious Galileans (referring to Christians, those who follow the "Galilean") support not only their own poor but ours as well, everyone can see that our people lack aid from us."[49] Oh, that such impious behaviour was still the mark of our rebellion.

The point is that when Jesus said "It shall not be so among you," he was not reprimanding us, he was declaring what *will be* when his disciples, reborn by and filled with the Holy Spirit, live the missional Kingdom culture he creates in them. We will be different. We will live a holy irrelevance that has the latent power to transform the world as we know it. E.R. Dodds, reflecting on the startling impact and growth of the church in the first three hundred years of her history, observes that the Christian success in creating a community that cared both for its own and for others was "a major cause, perhaps the strongest single cause, of the spread of Christianity."[50]

Desmund Tutu, a Nobel Peace Prize-winning bishop for his work during and after apartheid in South Africa, declared, "We have no option. We are servants of the God who reigns and cares. He wants us to be the alternative society..." How will we be the alternative society if we are only parroting the kingdom of this world and not bringing in the wild Kingdom of God with the way we live?

In 1982, the Miserete Kristos Church in Ethiopia, founded by the work of Mennonite missionaries who were primarily focused on community development in the mid-twentieth century, had five thousand members and watched helplessly as the communist regime imprisoned her leaders, drove out westerners, and confiscated church buildings and property. The startling result was the growth of the movement to fifty thousand believers over the next ten years. "Now we have a good, two-step plan for the growth of the church anywhere," joked a pastor, "Close down all the church buildings, and ask all the pastors to kindly take a long vacation!"[51]

---

[49] These quotes by Dionysius, Tertullian, Cyprian, and Julian are from Os Guinness, *Doing Well and Doing Good: Money, Giving, and Caring in a Free Society*, 128.
[50] Ibid. 129.
[51] Wolfgang Simson, *Houses That Change The World*, 171.

The same was and continues to be the reality in China. The relevance of the Christian community seen in their life together and great loving kindness is not dependent on church buildings, trendy programs, or professionals. Amazingly, the Chinese church permeates this holy irrelevance as an underground community. The Holy Spirit is the architect of a people who exist for the world our Lord came to save, and then end up living so wildly different that their world can't help but take notice.

Dietrich Bonhoeffer said, "The 'extraordinary'—and this is the supreme scandal—is something which the followers of Jesus *do*."[52] We don't just talk about what can be, we *are* what can be because God is at work in his people. Let the Kingdom come. A missional Kingdom culture lives the supreme scandal of actually doing the works of Jesus and living the extraordinary Kingdom of God on earth, just as it is hoped for in heaven. We don't just pray the Lord's Prayer; we expect to somehow be the answer to it. The holy irrelevance of the Church is the living reality that God is not irrelevant at all, but is for people and wants them to know his blessing and share his blessing with the world.

If we exist for the world our Lord came to save, how can our churches be wildly different and live a holy irrelevance?

First, by celebrating the extraordinary nature of the body of Christ. The church of every tribe, language, nation, and era is somehow God's way of communicating his wisdom to the world (Ephesians 3:10). In his death for all of us, Jesus broke down every barrier we might have erected between peoples (Ephesians 2:14f). When Christians realize this remarkable and hopeful truth and rally together around the cross and live that the Lamb might receive the reward of his suffering, a whole new vision of what can be is realized with vibrant tangibility.

Practically speaking, a church that seeks to love not just those who are like them should consider ways of establishing meaningful

---

[52] Dietrich Bonhoeffer, *The Cost of Discipleship*, 170-71.

two-way partnerships with other Christian communities of different ethnic, economic, and geographic situations. At Kingsfield-Zurich Mennonite Church, a rural predominately white band of disciples, we have built partnerships with Jane Finch Faith Community in Toronto and Brethren in Christ churches in Colombia. Kingsfield-Clinton is working on a similar partnership with believers in the Dominican Republic. Closer to home, our willingness to cross denominational lines would not only make our witness more relevant right where we live, but create opportunities to learn from the Spirit's work in the whole body of Christ.

In a world struggling with never-ending fragmentation, regional-ization, and tension, the church can demonstrate a wild difference because we know Jesus has made us a people where peace and love are not only possible, but meant to be shared. As Peter describes, *"But you are a chosen race, a royal priesthood, a holy nation, a people for his own possession, that you may proclaim the excellencies of him who called you out of darkness into his marvellous light ... Keep your conduct ... honorable, so that when they speak against you as evildoers, they may see your good deeds and glorify God on the day of visitation"* (1 Peter 2:9,12).

Second, by recovering our prophetic voice and presence in culture. Having spent so much time seeking to be relevant and liked in so many spheres, we have some work to do in remembering our voice and the necessity of our very peculiar presence.

Some Christians believe Jesus' voice is either politically left or politically right. In fact, he is neither and yet both. Beware! Just when we think we have him pinned, he will prove himself untamed. A redisc-overy of the prophetic voice will result in both the conservative right and liberal left loving and hating us at some point. We should always speak and act for the defense of the poor and oppressed, living and unborn, for the careful stewarding of creation, for the end of violence, while at the same time pointing only to Jesus as the ultimate hope for our deliverance from any of this. We speak the politics of Jesus. We speak of another land of which we are citizens. We are the present reality of a wild Kingdom and are committed to living it, even if we are persecuted and misunderstood.

To a church stuck in a cold war in the late twentieth century and trying to decide whose side God was on, Karl Barth bellowed, "There are no areas of which we can say: God has nothing to do here or this is none of God's business ... just as the whole is met with mercy, in the same way the whole is put under the discipline of grace."[53] So we offer the prophetic voice and point to the mercy and disciplining grace of the One True God, the untamed Lion of Judah who has business to do everywhere.

In the Franco-Prussian War of 1870-1871, the Quakers in the United Kingdom began The Friends War Victims Fund and sent volunteers to serve the wounded on both sides of the conflict. When World War I rolled around, and their caring precedent was already set, the Quakers immediately mobilized and sent some of their own to the front lines to investigate what was going on and how to respond. What they saw resulted in a mass appeal to the whole British Empire, "We find ourselves today in the midst of what may prove to be the fiercest conflict in the history of the human race. Whatever may be our view of the processes which have led to its inception, we have now to face the fact that war is proceeding on a terrific scale and that our own country is involved in it ... Our duty is clear: to be courageous in the cause of love and in the hate of hate."[54] They then proceeded to engage the war on both sides as lovers of the suffering, a servile reminder of the absurdity of the madness that had engulfed the "civilized" world. The prophetic voice of a wildly different people will be matched by a way of life that earns the right to speak.

A prophetic people don't speak and bury their heads in the sand. They seek to live what they speak. In word and deed, they translate God's Word into prophetic reality. When the first Mennonite settlers arrived in North America, they determined to have nothing to do with the slavery that permeated the "new world." One of their leaders, Peter Plockhoy, declared their prophetic stance, "No lordships or servile slavery shall burden our company."[55] Jesus words, "It shall not be so among you," is to be matched by our prophetic presence and lives that

---

[53] Quoted in Frank Jehle, *Ever Against the Stream*, 34.
[54] Donald F. Durnbaugh, *The Believer's Church*, 277.
[55] Ibid. 274-75.

bring the Kingdom of God into disturbing reality midst a dark and dying world.

Hence, it follows that one of the primary tasks of the church in a post-Christian culture will be the establishment and planting of more and diverse missional Kingdom communities. More churches must be started in neighbourhoods, burgs, boroughs, villages, towns, suburbs, and inner cities so that the prophetic voice of the church may be more profoundly felt, known, and seen in practice. The prophetic voice of the church must be felt in her active and multiplying presence among the peoples of the world. These churches, however, must be centered not just on programs or buildings of banal "relevance." They must be communities of prophetic presence, the intersection of real faith with real people and real life. New churches must clearly be a people set apart, set on fire, and sent on mission. Since the church is so wildly different, in fact a miracle, more churches of prophetic presence are needed to bring this miracle into tangible reality.

Third, by making obedience to the clear commands of God our number one priority. Mark Twain once quipped that it was not the stuff he didn't understand in Scripture that bothered him, it was the stuff he did understand that made him queasy. To live what has clearly been made known by God and commanded of us would dismantle almost every opposing voice that challenges the church. "True evangelical faith is of such a nature that it can not be workless or idle," wrote Menno Simons. *"If you love me,"* said Jesus, *"you will keep my commandments"* (John 14:15). True faith is argued with relevance by a holy irrelevant life of obedience. True faith believes that God has spoken in his Word, in the Word made flesh in Jesus Christ, and lives accordingly.

Faith is truth lived. And this is what makes it so wildly different in the world, for true faith lived is a constant and undeniable confession that God is, and he is powerful to save and transform. If anything other than obedience to Jesus, which spurred on the Moravians and so many others, is our priority, as churches we will immeasurably diminish and tarnish the presence of the Kingdom of God in our spheres of influence. We will make it impossible for patches of God-light to brighten the darkness and confusion of the age we are called to understand and exist for.

If Jesus' food, if what sustained him, was to do the will of the one who sent him and complete his work (John 4:34), then certainly our high missional task is as connected to obedience as his was. It is in the Son's obedient life to the Father that we see that God is for us. In his unflinching "Yes" to the Father, we see something wildly and attractively different than the drivel around us. The obedient life of the disciples of Jesus is no less potent.

Therefore, the powerful obedient life of the wildly different missional Kingdom culture ought to consist of these holy irrelevant qualities:

- Sheltering the widow and orphan (James 1:27).
- Avoiding favoritism (Acts 10:34; James 2:1).
- Caring for the poor (Leviticus 19:9-10; Galatians 2:10).
- Defending the oppressed, enslaved and abused (Isaiah 58).
- Meeting the needs of the hungry, sick, and imprisoned (Matthew 25:31-46).
- Fleeing from maliciousness, greed, idolatry, and sexual immorality of all kinds (1 Corinthians 6:9-11; 1 Thessalonians 4:3-8; 1 Timothy 6:3-11).
- Not seeking revenge or doing violence to others (Matthew 5:38-48; Romans 12:17-21).
- Reconciling conflicts and not suing other believers (Matthew 18:15-20; 1 Corinthians 6:1-8).
- Prioritizing and providing for family (Exodus 20:12; Ephesians 5:21-6:4; 2 Thessalonians 3:6-15).
- Sharing our money freely, happily, and generously (Malachi 3:6-12; Acts 2:45; 2 Corinthians 8:1-15).
- Submitting to government and social responsibility but obeying God first (Romans 13:1-7; Acts 5:27-32).
- Caring for and cherishing created life in all its forms (Genesis 1:28; Exodus 20:13; Deuteronomy 25:4; Matthew 6:26; Luke 6:35-36).

- Speaking truthfully (Zechariah 8:16-17; Matthew 5:37).
- Being willing to suffer for righteousness and the name of Christ (Matthew 5:11; Philippians 1:27).
- Loving good and hating evil (Romans 12:9).
- Resting from work and selfish striving (Exodus 20:8-11; Matthew 6:31-34; Mark 6:30-31).
- Working with joy and diligence (Colossians 3:22-25).

More could be drawn from the Scriptures, but suffice it to say that the obedient life really is wildly different than the world we see around us. Consider the unstoppable influence of disciples whose great joy and high call is to live these Kingdom qualities in this world our Lord came to save.

UPON FURTHER REVIEW...

- When have you experienced the church at its irrelevant best? Can you tell of a time when you realized just how beautifully different the church is in the world?
- What might the practices, structures, priorities, and worship gatherings of a missional people be like where disciples celebrate and are equipped for wild difference?
- Where does the prophetic voice of the disciples of Jesus need to be heard more courageously and compassionately in your community and culture?

FOR THE TOOLBOX

In building a growing capacity to answer the call to be a people who exist for the world our Lord came to save, the following tools can be effective aids in the healthy development of your missional Kingdom culture:

a. **Hit Reboot**
   The corporate discipline of Sabbath, of purposefully and wilfully resting and changing the pace of the life of your fellowship, can do wonders to reinvigorate and reenergize the call to join God on mission. Make no mistake, this is truly a discipline that goes beyond our Sunday "day of rest," which can actually be the most hectic day of all in the life of the local church. It takes great courage for a people to seriously take a break from their best-laid plans and seemingly holy busyness. When done well, a year or season spent refreshing the corporate batteries, opening up space for new dreams, and time to know one another in the family of God is beautiful beyond belief. For a biblical vision of the principles of Sabbath and Jubilee, read Leviticus 25 and Hebrews 4:1-13. A number of congregations, including Kingsfield-Zurich Mennonite Church, have creatively and bravely entered this rest and have many stories to tell. Search them out.

b. **Build Partnerships**
   Many churches already have partnerships with other believers in very different contexts through mission supports or past ministry relationships that have never been developed to their full potential. Formally forcing yourselves to commit to a creative *and* reciprocal partnership with believers not like you, whether domestic or international, should be at the heart of every missional congregation. These partnerships give wild difference a face and remind us thatthe world and God's Kingdom is much bigger than our backyard. It also deepens our love

for the world and pushes us outside our comfort zones. It can also thankfully disturb and reveal the callousness of our hearts and the unholy prejudices that yet linger. I personally believe that a church should have a meaningful partnership with another ministry *domestically*, though demographically different (i.e. rural/urban, white collar/inner city), and *internationally*, preferably where the language spoken is not your mother tongue. Anything that forces us to be in a situation where we are not in control, building trust, and entering with humility will teach us a great deal about ministry in our home settings and be full of shared blessing.

c. The "Bility" Triangle
Carson Pue, President of Arrow Leadership, shared this simple yet very helpful tool with my Arrow class. I have often gone back to it as a measure for whether our church fellowship is even able to exist for the world our Lord came to save. In other words, without knowing it, we can develop unhelpful emphases or habits that make us literally unable to exist rightly, even if our vision and mission statements are Pulitzer Prize winners. This diagram reminds us to keep the points of the triangle in balance, maintaining equilibrium, so that we truly have the corporate ability we hope and pray for.

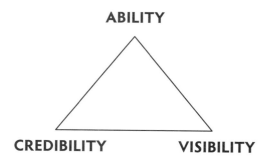

ABILITY

CREDIBILITY   **VISIBILITY**

Ability = What you can do. What gifts, abilities, resources, and opportunities are at your disposal as a people. These abilities will continually be developing, especially as disciples grow in Christ and realize their contributions to the Kingdom. Being honest about your abilities can help identify where further equipping is necessary and where your people have a unique contribution to share with your community that should not be taken for granted.

Credibility = Who you are. You might have many gifts to offer your community and world, but do you have a track record of bearing good fruit? Do people trust you? Do they know you well enough to decide? Again, this can grow, especially as you become known as a people who leave no one behind, have equipping leaders with vision, maturing disciples of character and perseverance, and a demonstrated love for the world.

Visibility = Where you go. You might have all the ability and credibility in the world, but if no one is ever touched by what God has done among you, what's it worth? Many congregations need the courage to grow in this area: to force themselves out of the comfy confines of their buildings, cliques, and well-crafted programs and be visible in flesh and blood in their communities. Our ability in these areas will grow, especially as the Spirit opens our eyes and hearts to the world our Lord came to save. Taking risky steps of increasing missional visibility beyond mere signage and building location is desperately needed by both the church and the world these days.

A PRAYER

At an international conference in Southeast Asia in 2005, underground Christians from China asked for prayer because of the tight restrictions their communist government had imposed. Their prayer requests centered on three main concerns: 1) no assembling of more than fifteen people was possible; 2) no unauthorized church buildings or sanctuaries were permitted; and 3) no unauthorized formal training of leaders was allowed.[56]

In other words, the underground churches of China are *forced* by an *atheistic* regime to multiply and spread, meet in homes and other small social settings, and train leaders from within rather than rely solely on separate institutions.

The church in China is a model of a missional Kingdom culture. Like the first century church, they are rapidly infiltrating and leavening their society in subversive and yeast-filled ways. They are truly salt and light. They understand that every believer is a missionary and church planter. Meanwhile, the privileged church of the northern and western world can gather freely in stadium-sized throngs, build new cathedrals to our hearts' content, and have for too long outsourced the responsibility of leadership development to institutions that risk detachment from the realities of the local church. Who, pray tell, has a brighter future?

We in the west should be troubled that they are praying for what we have. With great respect to these Chinese leaders who have suffered immensely for their faith, we should think soberly about praying with them in this regard. Instead, should we not pray together for the Kingdom to come in whatever way it must in both our contexts? Should our praying not more fully reflect that of the fledgling early church: *"Grant to your servants to continue to speak your word with all boldness,*

---

[56] Michael Frost, *Exiles,* 138.

while you stretch out your hand to heal, and signs and wonders are performed through the name of your holy servant Jesus" (Acts 4:29-30). This is prayer that rocks the household of God and shakes nations.

A missional Kingdom culture is foreign in this world. It is a multi-ethnic land with one grace-filled and untamed Lord. It is a Kingdom God initiates, but which human beings saved by grace and filled with the Holy Spirit embody. It is a Kingdom borne and sustained by prayer. We pray because we have to; there's just no other way for the Kingdom to come. We pray, as Jesus reminded his disciples during that fateful night on the Mount of Olives, so that we will not fall into temptation and miss the wild moves of the Holy Spirit (Luke 22:40). And so, with our brothers and sisters in China, we must be careful what we pray for—we just might get it in order that we might learn to pray more God-centered prayers next time around.

To send us as a people on mission with God—leaving no one behind, having leaders that lead, being disciples of Jesus who contribute to his Kingdom, and existing for the world our Lord came to save—let us really, honestly, desperately, thankfully, and selflessly pray:

> *Our Father in heaven,*
> *Hallowed be your name.*
> *Your kingdom come,*
> *Your will be done,*
> *On earth as it is in heaven.*
> *Give us this day our daily bread,*
> *And forgive us our debts,*
> *As we also have forgiven our debtors.*
> *And lead us not into temptation,*
> *But deliver us from evil.*
> MATTHEW 6:9-13

For yours, O Lord our God, is the Kingdom and the power and the glory, forever. And, our Living Lord, we desire to embody it already today. Amen.

Let the Kingdom Come...

BIBLIOGRAPHY

"Of making many books there is no end" (Ecclesiastes 12:12). The same applies to the vast horde of information available online, a cyber-expanse King Solomon could never have imagined.

I am humbled you have taken the time to read this meagre contribution to the overwhelming array of possible volumes at your disposal. What we choose to invest in and ingest should not be taken lightly or carelessly. As a guide to focus future reading, specifically as it relates to growing a missional Kingdom culture, the following selected list of historical and current authors and their work is provided to open your eyes and expand your vision. A number of websites and blogs are also provided for your surfing enjoyment. Many of these writers were quoted or referenced in this book. Others have been instrumental voices in forming, correcting, and sharpening my own growth as a disciple in a missional Kingdom culture. Enjoy!

Books

Adams, Michael. *Fire and Ice.* Toronto: Penguin, 2003.

Appleyard, Brian. *Understanding the Present.* New York: Doubleday, 1992

Barth, Karl. *Against the Stream.* London: SCM, 1954.

_____. *Community, State and Church.* Gloucester: Peter Smith, 1968.

_____. *Evangelical Theology.* Grand Rapids: Eerdmans, 1963.

_____. *The Christian Life.* Grand Rapids: Eerdmans, 1981.

Bonhoeffer, Dietrich. *Life Together.* San Francisco: Harper, 1954.

_____. *The Cost of Discipleship.* New York: MacMillan, 1963.

Bosch, David J. *Transforming Mission.* Maryknoll: Orbis, 1991.

Bruce, F.F. *The Spreading Flame.* Grand Rapids: Eerdmans, 1958.

Cavey, Bruxy. *The End of Religion.* Colorado Springs: NavPress, 2007.

BIBLIOGRAPHY

Chesterton, G.K. *Orthodoxy*. Garden City: Doubleday, 1959.

Cole, Neil. *Organic Church*. San Francisco: Jossey-Bass, 2005

Claiborne, Shane. *The Irresistible Revolution*. Grand Rapids: Zondervan, 2006.

Creps, Earl. *Off-Road Disciplines*. San Francisco: Jossey-Bass, 2006.

Dallaire, Romeo. *Shake Hands With the Devil*. Toronto: Knopf, 2003.

Dawn, Marva J. *A Royal Waste of Time*. Grand Rapids: Eerdmans, 1999.

DePree, Max. *Leadership Jazz*. New York: Dell, 1993

Driscoll, Mark. *The Radical Reformission*. Grand Rapids: Zondervan, 2004.

Durnbaugh, Donald F. *The Believer's Church*. Scottdale: Herald, 1968.

Dyck, Cornelius J., ed. *An Introduction to Mennonite History*. Scottdale: Herald, 1967.

Edwards, Jonathan. *Religious Affections*. Uhrichsville: Barbour, 1999.

Engel, James F., and William A. Dyrness. *Changing the Mind of Missions*. Downer's Grove: InterVarsity, 2000.

Estep, William R. *The Anabaptist Story*. Grand Rapids: Eerdmans, 1975.

Frost, Michael. *Exiles*. Peabody: Hendrickson, 2006.

___ and Alan Hirsch. *The Shaping of Things to Come*. Peabody: Hendrickson, 2003.

Ford, Leighton. *Transforming Leadership*. Downer's Grove: InterVarsity, 1991.

Gibbs, Eddie. *ChurchNext*. Downer's Grove: InterVarsity, 2000.

____. *LeadershipNext*. Downer's Grove: InterVarsity, 2005.

Gill, Robin. *Changing Worlds*. London: T&T Clark, 2002.

Guinness, Os. *Doing Well and Doing Good*. Colorado Springs: NavPress, 2001.

_____. *The Call*. Nashville: Word, 1998.

Hagberg, Janet O., and Robert A. Guelich. *The Critical Journey*. Salem: Sheffield, 2005.

Hauerwas, Stanley and William H. Willimon. *Resident Aliens*. Nashville: Abingdon, 1989.

Hedges, Chris. *I Don't Believe In Atheists*. New York: Free, 2008.

Hirsch, Alan. *The Forgotten Ways.* Grand Rapids: Brazos, 2006.

Horsch, John, trans. *Menno Simons' Life and Writings.* Scottdale: MPH, 1936.

Jeffrey, David Lyle, ed. *English Spirituality in the Age of Wesley.* Grand Rapids: Eerdmans, 1987.

Jenkins, Philip. *The Next Christendom.* Oxford: Oxford University Press, 2002.

Katongole, Emmanuel. *A Future for Africa.* Chicago: University of Chicago, 2005.

Kise, Jane A.G., David Stark, and Sandra Krebs Hirsh. *LifeKeys.* Minneapolis: Bethany, 1996.

Kouzes, James M., and Barry Z. Posner. *The Leadership Challenge.* San Francisco: Jossey-Bass, 2002.

Lewis, C.S. *The Screwtape Letters.* San Francisco: Harper, 1942.

_____. *Mere Christianity.* San Francisco: Harper, 1952.

_____. *The Lion, The Witch, And The Wardrobe.* London: Geoffrey Bles, 1950.

_____. *The Horse and His Boy.* London: Geoffrey Bles, 1954.

Lewis, Robert. *The Church of Irresistible Influence.* Grand Rapids: Zondervan, 2001.

Long, Jimmy. *Generating Hope.* Downer's Grove: InterVarsity, 1997.

McLaren, Brian D. *A New Kind of Christian.* San Francisco: Jossey-Bass, 2001.

Milbank, John. *Theology & Social Theory.* Malden: Blackwell, 1990.

Neill, Stephen. *A History of Christian Missions.* London: Penquin, 1990.

Newbigin, Lesslie. *The Open Secret.* Grand Rapids: Eerdmans, 1978.

_____. *Foolishness to the Greeks.* Grand Rapids: Eerdmans, 1986.

_____. *The Gospel In A Pluralist Society.* Grand Rapids: Eerdmans, 1989.

Newton, John. *Spiritual Letters on Growth and Grace.* Public domain, 1772.

Noll, Mark. *Turning Points.* Grand Rapids: Baker, 1997.

Pelikan, Jaroslav. *The Excellent Empire.* San Francisco: Harper, 1987.

Pue, Carson. *Mentoring Leaders.* Grand Rapids: Baker, 2005.

Roxburgh, Alan J., and Fred Romanuk. *The Missional Leader.* San Francisco: Jossey-Bass, 2006.

Sanders, Oswald. *Spiritual Leadership.* Chicago: Moody, 1967.

Scazzero, Peter. *The Emotionally Healthy Church.* Grand Rapids: Zondervan, 2003.

Sider, Ronald J. *Rich Christians In An Age Of Hunger.* Downer's Grove: InterVarsity, 1977.

____. *The Scandal of the Evangelical Conscience.* Grand Rapids: Baker, 2005.

Simson, Wolfgang. *Houses That Change The World.* Emmelsbull: C & P Publishing, 1999.

Stanley, Paul D. and J. Robert Clinton. *Connecting.* Colorado Spring: Navpress, 1992.

Taylor, Charles. *A Secular Age.* Cambridge: Belknap, 2007.

Tiplady, Richard. *Postmission.* Cumbria: Paternoster, 2003.

Tolkien, J.R.R. *The Lord of the Rings: The Return of the King.* London: HarperCollins, 1999.

Volf, Misoslav and William Katerberg, ed. *The Future of Hope.* Grand Rapids: Eerdmans, 2004.

Willard, Dallas. *The Spirit of the Disciplines.* San Francisco: Harper, 1988.

____. *Renovation of the Heart.* Colorado Springs: NavPress, 2002.

Yoder, John Howard. *The Politics of Jesus.* Grand Rapids: Eerdmans, 1972.

Yoder Neufeld, Thomas R. *Recovering Jesus.* Grand Rapids: Brazos, 2007.

Websites, Blogs, and Vlogs

www.theresurgence.com

www.theresurgence.com/md_blog (Mark Driscoll blog)

www.missionalchurchnetwork.com

www.allelon.org (movement of missional leaders)

www.theforgottenways.org (Alan Hirsch blog)

www.forgecanada.ca or www.forge.org.au (Missional Training Network)

www.theo-phil-us.blogspot.com (Phil Wagler blog)

www.thirdway.com (Mennonite Media)

www.mennonitechurch.ca/resources/missional/ (Mennonite Church Canada's missional church travel bag)

www.mennonitemission.net/Resources/Publications/MissionalLens/ (Mennonite Church USA's "Through a Missional Lens")

www.leadershipjournal.net

www.blog.christianitytoday.com/outofur/ (Out of Ur—a blog of
ChristianityToday.com)

www.acts29network.org

www.wordpress.com (one of the more interesting smorgasbords on
the blogosphere)

www.mypeopleinternational.com (Aboriginal Christians on mission)

www.smallboatbigsea.org (home page of missiologist Michael Frost's
church)

www.redeemer.com (home page of Redeemer Presbyterian Church in
New York City, one of North America's most rapidly multiplying
churches, led by Tim Keller)

www.cole-slaw.blogspot.com (Neil Cole blog)

www.deliberatesimplicity.blogspot.com (Dave Browning blog—
founding pastor of Christ the King Community Church,
International)

www.anabaptistnetwork.com (network of churches in the United
Kingdom and Ireland)

www.thesimpleway.org/shane/ (Shane Claiborne blog)

www.rickmckinley.net (Rick McKinley blog)

Many of these websites provide links to other helpful contributors
and resources as well.

ABOUT THE AUTHOR

Phil Wagler is lead pastor of Kingsfield, a multiplying movement of churches in Huron County, Ontario. Phil and his wife Jen are blessed with four children: Caleb, Benjamin, Jessie, and Sadie. Together they have served God's Kingdom in local church, denominational, and college settings in Canada and internationally. He writes regularly for magazines and websites in Canada and the United States. Phil is a graduate of Emmanuel Bible College, Tyndale Seminary, the Arrow Leadership Program, and the school of life. He was named among 35 Canadian leaders under the age of 35 in the National Recognition Project of 2007.

He can be contacted at phil_wagler@yahoo.ca. You can also get in touch by telephone—(519) 236-4933—or by snail mail, at Box 5, Zurich, Ontario, N0M 2T0.